The Leader's Toolbox

# ADVANCED PRAISE FOR
# THE LEADER'S TOOLBOX

Thank you, thank you, thank you. Your training was the breath of fresh air needed to restore and renew my journey as a manager. The information gained is readily applicable and it will work! The rest is on me to execute! Keep up the great work!

— **Terri Cross**, *Client Success Manager*

I started my HR team meeting today with P.O.W. — at which point, one of my team members said "Oh wow, this is unexpected and new…this is cool, I Love it"

— **Stacy Wade**, *Chief People Officer*

Thank you for your passion and commitment to your craft. It was perceived through the screen. My team was extremely thankful for your time, it has sparked many fruitful conversations. My goal has always been to win hearts and minds to achieve long-lasting performance, it's impactful to see someone do that (in you) on a high level.

— **VP** *at Certa ProPainters*

I am in awe. My students spoke to you more in one hour than they have spoken to me in the last two weeks. Really. They absolutely adored you, and your words resonated more deeply with them than anything I've seen before. After you left, they all downloaded your app. Thank you a million times for being such a fantastic person and for sharing some time with us.

— **Shani Cater**, *Professor at Wagner College*

# THE
# LEADER'S
# *TOOLBOX*

### *Tools to* EVOLVE *Your Leadership*

... and that of those you're leading!

## ANDRE YOUNG

NEW YORK

LONDON • NASHVILLE • MELBOURNE • VANCOUVER

# THE LEADER'S *TOOLBOX*

Tools to EVOLVE your Leadership … and that of those you're leading

Published in New York, New York, by Morgan James Publishing. Morgan James is a trademark of Morgan James, LLC. www.MorganJamesPublishing.com

Proudly distributed by Ingram Publisher Services.

A **FREE** ebook edition is available for you
or a friend with the purchase of this print book.

_____

CLEARLY SIGN YOUR NAME ABOVE

**Instructions to claim your free ebook edition:**
1. Visit MorganJamesBOGO.com
2. Sign your name CLEARLY in the space above
3. Complete the form and submit a photo of this entire page
4. You or your friend can download the ebook to your preferred device

ISBN 9781631959233 paperback
ISBN 9781631959240 ebook
Library of Congress Control Number:
2022935542

**Cover Design by:**
Rachel Lopez
www.r2cdesign.com

**Interior Design by:**
Chris Treccani
www.3dogcreative.net

Morgan James is a proud partner of Habitat for Humanity Peninsula and Greater Williamsburg. Partners in building since 2006.

Get involved today! Visit MorganJamesPublishing.com/giving-back

# ACKNOWLEDGMENTS

I am blessed to have so many people and experiences in my life to be grateful for. Thank you to my family and friends for your support, encouragement, inspiration, and wisdom.

Love and honor to my beautiful wife, Sarah, for your unlimited devotion through the happiest and toughest times of my life. Thank you for all that you are and for all that you do. To my children: Xiomara, André, Mason, and Sky. I love you! I am complete with you all in my life.

To my Dad, thank you for being my calming rock. Your words, sincerity, and patience continue to leave me in awe. To my brother, Randy, I love you til the end. Many, many thanks to my other family members and friends who support me, keep me grounded, and add to the man and leader I continuously get to become. Lastly, to my Mom; this book is especially dedicated to you! She passed away on February 10, 2021, but her lessons will never die. Thank You for modeling and teaching the importance of being willing and able to listen to ANYTHING and EVERYTHING. It's amazing what you'll hear and learn from your people when they know they can come to you and trust you! Thanks Mom, and Rest in Peace. We love you!

Lastly, a special thanks to my friend Ed Burns. Thank you for supporting my vision so many years ago; recommending I start writing three blogs per week to boost my SEO's. Your suggestion has led to four books and an unstoppable passion and ability I didn't know I possessed. A BIG Thank YOU!

# CONTENTS

**A Leader's Passion ... Plus: Leadership takes passion; plus a few more things!**                                      **113**

# The 5 Points of Your Day!

As you begin The Leader's Toolbox, it's important to start
here! I'm honored so many organizations worldwide reach
out to me seeking to impact their leaders and employees; eager
to enhance their people's professional leadership, daily leadership
skills, and lives outside of work. I'll share with you, just as I share
with them ... It's imperative to start trainings ... and this book ...
with The 5 Points of Your Day! If you want to live the life of your
dreams, professionally and personally ... and enhance your Leadership & Work/Life Harmony ... this is the foundation! Remember, everyone has 24 hours in a day; leaders use theirs differently.
Let's jump in!

**Point 1: What You Consume When You Wake Up!**

Sorry ... there's no fancy name for Point 1! You may be thinking about what you eat or your diet, but that's not what I mean.

Please, by all means, eat healthy; as we only get one life to live. However, I'm referring to what you put in your mind and spirit when you first wake up!

I often hear from leaders and employees they wake up grabbing their phone, iPad, or laptop and take it to the bathroom to check and respond to emails. As an employer, it may seem impressive and you may want hundreds or thousands of employees like this. As an employee, it may seem like a logical way to get a jump on the day. However, compound this act … day after day, month after month, year after year, decade after decade … how'd you think you'd end up feeling about your job … starting your day complaining about an email, who sent it, how dumb someone is, or a sharp email that grinds your gears before you've gotten a chance to even brush your teeth … Be Mindful!

So, since you're not starting your day by checking your email or scrolling social media; what to do instead? The answer is, anything that enhances your positivity, your passion, and your production professionally and personally! During my last job as an employee … a coworker came to me and said, "You know how you have one of those bad mornings?". I thought carefully as I didn't want to come across cocky. The truth is, I haven't had a bad morning since 2011. I've had busy mornings with having three young kids back then. I've had mornings I'd rather stay in bed, but I haven't had a bad morning since 2011 … Why? When I started my business in 2011, I'd go to bed every night looking for positive quotes to post in the morning. When I woke up, I came up with a question related to the quote.

As time passed, I started making personal development and leadership videos in the morning and finding short motivational videos to watch. Years of this have made it impossible for me to have a bad morning! Whatever your process, it simply starts to become who you are! So, be mindful of what you consume when you wake up. For me, it's short motivational videos and posting my content. Perhaps yours will be the same ... or meditation, prayer, push-ups, or quiet time with your coffee before the rest of the world is up. Whatever it is ... be sure it's making you better, not bitter!

**Point 2: Organize Your Day!**

It's no wonder leaders and employees are so on edge; as you attempt to maintain order of the tornado of things you have to do in a day ... I like to say "Get to do", but you get the point! Organizing your day means you keep a notebook by your computer or wherever you get your work done ... with the purpose of writing your list of "Things to Do". It's important to get what's in your head on paper. My list tends to average 15-20 things daily for me to run my business effectively.

As a leader, be sure your list is making you "Better" not just "Busy". Before I pull the covers back in the morning and my feet hit the floor, I say two things to myself. "Let's be great and have some fun today" ... I'll explain more about this later in the book. The second thing is a question, "What are my wins for the day?". Having an answer to this question will give your day purpose and allow you to win the day instead of the day beating you! When you make your list ... be sure your wins are at the very top; allowing you to cross off wins that propel you, your team, and your organization forward!

Organizing your day also involves who you choose to associate with at work. As a leader ... you walk in with your head up, eyes up, smiling, greeting, and saying hello to everyone; but you don't park it and live there with everyone! You know the Negative Nicks

& Nacys, Gossipers, and Grouches ... be gracious to everyone and keep it moving!

**Point 3: Relationship Building and Self-Care!**

Let's start with Self-Care! No matter how much you love what you do for a living; at some point in the day, we all hit a wall. For some, it may be one o'clock, two o'clock, or whenever ... it's coming! When it happens, it's time to do something good for YOU. For me, it's remembering to eat. I love what I get to do for a living and get consumed by it and can easily forget to eat! Perhaps it's taking a walk, eating with new people, scrolling positive things and people you subscribe to on your phone. Whatever it is, enjoy it!

You'll find Relationship Building to be a gift ... for you and your loved ones! What would it take for you to send a nice text to your significant other midday? Not much, right? My wife and I both work from home and from time to time I send her a nice text ... even though she's right upstairs, "Hey Beautiful, I hope your day is going as amazing as you are! I love You!". Believe me, it sets up the back half of my day very nicely! Maybe you decide to send a nice text to your parents if you're still lucky enough to have them ... your kids, your friends. Let's be real, we all have the fastest texting thumbs on the planet; let's put them to good use! I think we all can spare 20 seconds to gift your partner, parents, kids, friends, and your life!

**Point 4: How You Return Home!**

If you're reading this book; I'm assuming you're in a professional position of leadership or would like to be. So here's a question ... Would you ever purposely hire someone that looked as if they were dragging themselves around, complaining all the time, and looking as if they'd rather be anywhere else? I hope your answer is "No". Then isn't it a shame that's how most of us return home after a day at work … or to the living room after closing the laptop? Dragging ourselves through the door, complaining about the day, your boss, your employees, and everything in between. Let's be mindful of how we return home and gift our family with the same energy you'd want your employees to exhibit walking through the door or clicking onto a Virtual Call!

The key is to know what you need, so you can return home like a leader. For me, it was going to the gym after work; it was the only place where it was ALL ABOUT ME for an hour. It also gave me my second wind and I could return home happy to put my cape on and become Superman, Superhusband, and Superdad! For you, perhaps it's a shower, a walk, or 15 minutes of personal chill-time. Whatever it is … BE SURE you're a better person after doing it … this makes it easier for the people in your life to accept what you're doing … and they will actually want you to do it because they enjoy how you are and who you are when you return!

**Point 5: "What was my Biggest Accomplishment of the Day?"**

Monday through Friday, before I close my eyes to go to sleep, I ask myself this question … and I implore you to do the same! It's one of the most powerful questions you can ever ask yourself and having an answer to this question will allow you to have won the day, instead of the day consistently kicking your butt. I hear from so many people, especially women, that they lay in bed at night thinking of all the things they didn't get done and ALL the things they have to do the next day. Do you know how much you actually did and accomplished today … and everyday? Your brain is faster than you think and I promise you will have an answer to this question … and most likely more than one! In this quiet time of reflection, give yourself a pat on the back for your Biggest

Accomplishment of the day ... and for all of the small ones no one may know about!

To take it a bit further, ask your significant other ... your kids. I guarantee you don't know their answer! My wife works in land development ... I have no idea what she's talking about when she discusses the grading of land and swales (I hope I spelled it right) ... however, when I ask her this question, I know what to hug her for, what to say congrats about, what to celebrate with her, that I'm proud of her, and great job Baby!

This is the 5 Points of Your Day! Notice, it's not a lot of time out of your day. It's about intent and consistency! You do this consistently, not just when you're motivated on a Monday or January 1st, and you will evolve professionally and personally! Before you move on in this book to learn concepts to put in your Leader's Toolbox, answer this quick question ... What was your Biggest Takeaway from the 5 Points ... which point resonated with you that you will make a homework assignment for yourself RIGHT NOW? Remember ... knowing something new, without applying that something new, will lead to nothing new!

*"Everyone has 24 hours in a day; leaders use theirs differently"*
– Andre Young

A Leader's People

*Evolving Your Leadership and
That of Those You're Leading*

# CHAPTER 1

# A Leader's Ingredients; The 4 Ingredients to Build Successful Teams, Leaders, & Organizations!

Ask anyone who knows me and they'll tell you; cooking isn't my thing! I don't enjoy the ratio of time it takes to prepare and clean; compared to the time it takes to eat. However, I was lucky to marry my wife ... she loves to cook and bake and is the best at both! Although I dislike cooking, I do know the ingredients to become and help others become great leaders. Whether professionally, athletically, or personally ... it's always the same four ingredients: Talent, Work Ethic, Coaching, and Opportunity. If you're interested in furthering your journey as a leader and building your team and your organization, keep reading!

## Talent

Let's face it, some people's ambition outweighs their talent. Have you ever met someone, worked with someone, or was that someone that had all the drive, but struggled to have the talent to succeed to their desired level? I was that person as an athlete. My ambition was high and it allowed me to play college football and make an Arena Football team however, I lasted about five minutes with the New England Patriots scouts! Have you ever met, worked with, or been the person whose talent outweighed their ambition … they had all the talent in the world, but a low or inconsistent effort level? It's truly a sad thing to see; as everyone but them knows their effort level is the problem!

The truth is, some people are born with innate ability and personality to achieve in the area they desire and some have to work ten times harder for the same opportunity. The good thing is, talent can be enhanced and it's not the only ingredient of success and leadership!

Even those with a natural talent for the path they desire must choose to refine it; here are some tips:

- Study your craft! Read books, articles, YouTube Videos, anything you can get your hands on to learn more, be more, and add to your toolbox!

- What is your Superpower? Know what you bring to the table regarding your talent … and hone it!

- Ask the Get Great Question! Most people will focus on enhancing what they're already good at. However, if it's not impacting your organization, boss, or team the way they want and need most … you're simply busy being busy! Leaders understand the benefit of marrying what they want to do, and what they want to give … with what the people receiving it need most right now! So, know your talent and marry it to your company's needs … and everyone wins!

**Work Ethic**

Leaders understand without work ethic … great talent can be frustrating and sometimes useless. A talented lazy person can be as frustrating to have on your team as a motivated untalented person. Work Ethic means you're willing to consistently set aside time to evolve your skills. Perhaps it's keeping up to date with your profession as it evolves, staying up to date with how your clients prefer your product, reading 15 mins every evening, taking classes, attending trainings, or working on a new move if you're an athlete. Whatever it is … leaders don't succumb to the "Hamster Wheel" or the day-to-day grind of simply getting stuff done. They make consistent time to grow and evolve!

**Coaching**

We can only go so far alone and coaching will take you and your people to the next level. I once had lunch with a gentleman and was enlightened by how simple he explained coaching. He asked me to raise my hand … I did. Then he said, "raise it higher" … and I did! We may be doing all we think we can do until we are asked to do a bit more, learn something new, or shown a new perspective our mindset would have never considered. If you are looking to enhance your leadership or your success … I highly recommend a coach or mentor; allowing you to enhance your skills, perspective, and impact.

When you're in a professional position of leadership, your job is to be a mentor and coach! Remember, managers crack the whip from behind and simply tell others what to do; taking care of the busy and day-to-day. Leaders build other leaders by coaching, explaining the bigger picture, enhancing skill-sets, complimenting, having the tough conversations with constructive insight, and motivating your people in their language toward success!

My youngest son plays quarterback and his dream is to play at a Division I University then the NFL. He has the talent, has the work ethic, he practices on his off-days, and then asks to practice again with me afterward. Due to this, it's now my job to get him the proper coaching to take him to the next level ... starting off small with YouTube Videos to mimic, to official Quarterback Coaching Sessions, traveling to attend camps, making connections, and more! The people in your organization and on your team have the talent and the work ethic ... What are you doing, professionally, to best coach them? It helps to know what they want to get out of working with you and for you? What's their definition of professional success? What help would they like most from you right now?

When what they need and want is reasonable, doable, and fair for the organization and you ... do it a bit outside of your comfort zone; enhancing your leadership, but not your bitterness and frustration level! When what they need and want is outside your boundaries, it makes sense to be transparent and clear about it and provide possible alternatives while maintaining high expectations and standards toward the mission and job at hand!

## Opportunity

The fourth ingredient ... Opportunity! When you and your people have honed their talent, demonstrated consistent work ethic, and have benefited from coaching; opportunities will arise!

When you're in a leadership position, the ingredient of opportunity can be sweet and sometimes bittersweet. As you've recruited great talent, honed their talent, they've exhibited work ethic, and you've provided top-level coaching ... your people will desire opportunity. They may want that promotion, raise, autonomy to make decisions on their own, and more ... and why wouldn't they; it's the next logical step!

The truth is, your organization or team has improved because your people have improved, but there are only so many spots for promotions and there's only so much money to go around. There may not be enough opportunity to go around and not everyone who started with you will end with you. This sounds awful ... and it's sad, however a great problem to have. So, what to do?

I'd like to say it's a Win-Win-Win! It is a win that your people are becoming their definition of success, better leaders, and your organization is winning as individuals are provided opportunities to advance ... A Win! Some will be unable to advance the way they'd like and will choose to stay within an awesome organization ... although disappointed, they understand not everyone can move up or win all at the same time ... A Win! Other great people will decide to leave and seek opportunities elsewhere. It sounds bad, however it's great ... as your organization becomes a beacon and a Gold-Star to have on a resume. Your organization is now the Gold-Standard representing a place that puts out great people, a great place to work; if not for its reputation but also for the experience it will provide. Losing great people isn't the worse thing ... as long as you're losing them for the right reasons and have a reputation and system in place to attract more ... A Win!

Lastly, and very important to note, organizations and teams have traditionally looked at the ingredients I've shared as something an employee has to earn. For example, when an employee exhibits great talent and work ethic; the organization will then reward them with coaching and opportunity. I'm suggesting a powerful and evolving shift to impact the future of your company, your people, and your leadership ... Provide all of your people, regardless of their current talent level and work ethic with tremendous coaching, make opportunities clear and obtainable, and watch more of your people's talent rise and their work-ethic increase!

Also, many organizations will invest in their C-Suite, Middle Management, and Emerging Leaders; and rightfully so. However, many employees are being neglected and missing out on valuable Leadership & Work/Life Harmony Trainings that can impact their lives and your organization moving forward when learned early! Front-Line employees may not need all of the training C-Suite, Middle Management, and Emerging Stars get; but since you will most likely promote from within, it makes sense they get some … Be Mindful!

> *"When you raise your value, you raise your standard of opportunity."*
> – Andre Young

# CHAPTER 2

A Leader's Definition; Become the
Leader Your Team Needs!

Some were born with natural leadership skills, some lead when the situation calls for it, and others don't prefer leadership's spotlight at all. None of these positions on being a leader are right, wrong, positive, or negative ... it's people, their preferences, and how they see themselves. Whether you're in a professional position of leadership at your work, the janitor, or simply living your life, it's important to know ... you can be a leader if you choose to be!

I encourage you first to define what leadership means to you. Too many times, people chase without defining. Whatever dream, goal, or vision you desire ... start by specifically defining what it is. Knowing the specifics allow you to know when you've won and when to celebrate! Leading a team is not for the faint of heart. Some will jump in with both feet; while others will toe-test. Either way is a start and an opportunity to propel you further than you were yesterday. So, what's my definition of leadership?

I define leadership in 5 words: influence, impact, protection, decide, and expectations. When done consistently, these simple, yet powerful words will enhance not only your Leadership & Work/Life Harmony but also impact those around you; creating win-wins!

## Influence

Leaders positively influence others toward the direction of the desired vision and goal. Leaders know the way and show the way … leading from the front; rather than cracking the whip from the back. Your people must respect and trust you; the only way that happens is when they see you leading from the front. To do so … you must know, share, and influence the Vision!

Too often, I meet with organizations, executives, and coaches who are unaware or unclear of their vision for the company or team. When you don't know … how can your people? How can you maintain expectations? How will you know when you've won?

## Impact

Be of Impact! Think of a past boss or coach that positively impacted your life. Perhaps it was something they said, something they taught you, how they disciplined you (we all need a butt-kicking from time to time). Do you remember them? Will you be this person for someone 5, 10, 20 years from now?

Be of impact … you never know what action will do this, but locking yourself in your office and not engaging with others won't get it done. Coming home from work complaining about your day and retreating to your bedroom for the rest of the night won't get it done. Griping about the "Have-To's" of your day and looking as if you'd rather be anywhere else other than your job or home won't get it done. Be Mindful!

**Protection**

This is my favorite word of leadership and the one that's most often forgotten. As leaders, it's our job to protect! There will be times you must protect your people from themselves and their bad habits. You know who is habitually late, misses deadlines, and all of the other bad habits that have a negative impact. Protecting people from themselves means you set high expectations and standards, know and enforce the rules, and follow through.

As leaders, we also must be willing to protect our people from us! You know when you're having a bad day and it's not the best time to have that difficult conversation, you know that employee or person in your life that will always say "Yes"; allowing you to burn them out. It's your job as a leader to be more self-aware and understand … just because you can doesn't mean you should!

Lastly, as a leader, we must protect our time. Your time is important and it's imperative you organize your day to the best of your ability before the day starts and/or have time slots designated for the week to lead others with non-emergency issues, meetings, and follow-ups. Otherwise, you become a professional "Mr. Fix or Ms. Fix-It" all day long, putting out every fire, getting nothing done; training followers instead of building leaders. Remember, leaders build other leaders!

**Decide**

As a leader, when you're clear on your Vision … it makes it easier to know what to say "Yes" and "No " to. When you decide, be sure to be clear, optimistic, have your people in the right seat to maximize their superpower, and be willing to let the process evolve as necessary.

Although this is important … the decision I'm referring to is your decision to enter your work, your relationships, and your life with your head up, eyes up, smiling, willing to DO your best, and BE your best! When you can positively connect with the people in your life, professionally & personally, know your craft better than those around you, and are your best consistently ... it's amazing who will follow, how much more your people will do for you and with you, and how much they'll forgive when you mess up!

## Expectations

A leader that sets no expectations or consequences will not be leading for long! I'm very oppositional by nature and even writing the word rules or consequences makes me cringe a bit. However, the truth is, when you don't have rules you cannot and will not achieve your vision as a team. Simply put, a vision without expectations is just hope; and expectations without consequences are merely suggestions. You're suggesting people do a good job, show up on time, meet deadlines, follow through on things discussed, and treat coworkers and customers properly.

Now you know my definition of leadership. I hope it resonates with you; taking all of it or pieces of it to enhance your leadership and work/life harmony and that of those on your team. Enjoy your evolution!

*"As a leader, when you're clear on your Vision ... it makes it easier to know what to say "Yes" and "No" to!"*
— Andre Young

# CHAPTER 3

# A Leader's 3 P's; The 3 Prerequisites for Your Employees ... and Your Leaders!

Have you ever shopped at a store and when it was time to be served it was as if the employee was angry at you for making them do their job ... or aggravated they had to stop their conversation with their coworker to assist you? Or, my favorite ... the no eye contact, no smile, no greeting, their employer must have dragged them to work at gunpoint to help you type of service? It always leaves me wondering, how did this person get the job? Who else was interviewing that this person was the best option? And, what's the plan to improve and upgrade the hiring process, the training process, and standards?

As an organization, pickings may be slim regarding the number of employees who want to work, want to work for you, and bodies are sometimes hired to keep everything afloat to satisfy massive growth; but please remember ... who you bring in + what you expect + what you tolerate = your culture! These negative experiences, mixed with the wonderful employee experiences I've encountered, made it simple for me to know the 3 BIG P's I was looking for when I started bringing people into my business years ago. So, what are they?

**Positive**

Anyone I hired in the past, outsource with now, or partner with must be Positive! I define positive as having their head up, eyes up, smiling, upbeat, creative, willing to learn, they possess initiative, and in general when they walk into a room … the room is uplifted and people are better for having them around. As a leader, it's important to understand everyone will have their bad day … even you … due to organizational issues, personal issues, sometimes customer/client issues. Leaders bounce back quicker and better than everyone else and that's the positivity you're looking for!

I once worked in a very demanding facility where the work was tough, but very rewarding. I was a Mental Health Therapist, and I took pride in our building and the culture we created … too bad our leadership didn't. When employees of the company that worked outside of our building did a bad job, who were the opposite of "Positive", or simply burnt-out they weren't let go or mandated to attend proper trainings … they were relocated to our building to either burn-out further and quit or disappear into the abyss. Can you believe that? Needless to say, these individuals, although good people, were not positive and not happy about the move to the "Dreaded Place", and it showed as they looked miserable interacting with our clients, led nothing, and exacerbated many volatile situations making it harder for everyone else!

Bringing in Positive people is key; as they will be the face of your organization, your leadership, and a model for your clients and customers as well. I love getting to speak and train around the world and even when attendees in the crowd have masks on (due to Covid protocols), I can still tell the "Positive" people by their eyes … it's a truly amazing thing. Inherently, these Positive people sometimes approach me afterward and ask if they can have a job within my company. It's an overwhelming honor and I wish I could hire them all; instead I may provide them coaching and/ or connect them with companies I know are Positive and would allow them the opportunity, culture, and growth they're seeking! Remember, Positivity is great … however one "P" without the other two doesn't work!

**Passionate**

Positivity can take you far, while Passion + Positivity is like hitting the Nitro Button! I laugh as I write this because I know nothing about cars. However, I do know when I'm at the arcade with my kids and we play the car racing game and I hit that Nitro Button … ZOOOOOM … off I go! Passionate means, not only are your people positive, they also care about the work they're doing … they believe in it at their core or at the least, the good it will do for the organization, client/customer, and the world!

When I hired my Virtual Assistant, I had the privilege of interviewing three candidates. They were all wonderful and I asked my 7 Leader's Interview Questions to them individually. When it came down to the questions, "What's your Dream?", "What do you like most about the job?", and "What do you like least about your job?" one person stood out above the rest! Two candidates had other professional aspirations and wanted, or needed, a job and there's nothing wrong with that … I've been there. However, one candidate stated … with the passion … she loved helping people see their dreams come true and enjoyed being a part of the journey! She also shared her dreams of running her own business and that the worst part of her job was not knowing what was expected of her because she wanted to be great at what she did and that's not possible without great leadership. I'd like to thank the world's best Virtual Assistant, Nichole, for all of the behind-the-scenes stuff it takes to run a business and literally getting me to where I need to be around the globe, helping me to lead, being positive, passionate, and the final P…

**Productive**

Being Positive and Passionate without being Productive will not work! At the end of the day, business and leadership is about results! Can you … and will you … do what you said you were going to do and beyond? My job is to over-deliver! Most organizations have hesitations about bringing in a "so-called" Professional Speaker or Leadership Trainer … as would I. Unless you know them or they're a huge name like Tony Robbins, you have no idea what you're getting. Productive means you get the job done, you follow through, people and the organization can trust you, and you've made your name synonymous with your craft!

However, beware … Productive isn't meant to stand alone. I'm sure you've worked with an individual that was productive, but they weren't Positive … I have! For example, their sales numbers are through the roof; however they cheated their coworkers, stole clients, bullied customers/clients, etc. Terrell Owens, former NFL superstar wide receiver, may be the best example of this. He was ultra-productive everywhere he went, was one of the best wide receivers of all time … and is struggling to get into the NFL Football Hall-of-Fame because he was Productive and Passionate … but wasn't Positive. He broke apart locker rooms, teams, and became an intentional distraction … making everything all about him everywhere he went until team after team decided Production wasn't enough and it'd be best for him to take his singular "P" of Production elsewhere!

As a leader, are you being Positive, Passionate, and Productive? Not only in the ways you want to be; but also marrying it with the ways your people, team, and organization need most from you right now? As a Front-Line Employee, are you being Positive, Passionate, and Productive? Not only in the ways you want to be; but marrying it with the ways your leaders, team, and organization need most from you right now? It's not only about doing and being The 3 P's when you start, or when you're motivated on a Monday, on January 1st as a New Year's Resolution, or when things are going your way ... this is an ongoing expectation and the specific exception within my Leader's 3 of having a Vision & Vision Factors, Expectations, and Rules ... we'll get into this more in Chapter 5. Model the P's as a leader, Expect the P's from your people, and Enjoy you're your professional and personal evolution!!!

> *"Who you bring in + What you expect + What you tolerate =*
> *your culture ... Be Mindful!"*
> – Andre Young

# CHAPTER 4

---

# A Leader's Interview; The 7 Questions that Enhance Your Leadership & Excite Candidates!

Over the years, I've had the honor of hiring awesome people into my company, my dream, my baby! It was easy to be attracted to the "Inspired & Motivated", wide-eyed, eager candidate that struggled to blink as you spoke; as you could see your words and mission enter their soul ... I call that "Vacuum -Eyes"! We all want candidates this eager! As I've evolved ... so have the questions I ask and encourage you to ask when interviewing to add great people to your organization or team. So, what are they?

Before the questions and conversation start, I must say, the power of making eye contact, smiling, and a positive attitude goes a long way! I've found many candidates are doing their best to manage the tornado of emotions swirling inside: anxiety to say the right answer, stress because they really want or really need the job, intimidation as they meet with a person in a position of leadership, or frustration; as this may be their tenth interview. Whatever their tornado, let's kick off the experience with a warm greeting, eye contact, and a smile.

My favorite intro is … "Happy Monday (or whatever day it is)" and simply asking the candidate "How's your day so far". This is not one of the 7 Questions, but still monumentally important! Have you ever asked someone, "How's your day" and they respond "living the dream" with a flat affect and dragging themselves around, "It's too cold outside", "Too hot", or "Too whatever"? The candidate may have all of the skills, however, not the mindset you choose to build with and add to your organization, vision, and team. This question tends to be a great starting point … Be Mindful!

**Question 1**

*How long have you been doing this?*

Whether they say forty days or forty years … It can give a quick gauge of experience level; no answer is wrong. Some employers prefer a higher level of time on a job and experience; however, the concern is the candidate may be set in their ways or struggle to learn new things. While other employers don't mind minimal experience and are willing to make mistakes together to teach what needs to be known.

More and more companies are hiring based on the PERSON and have a Company University to Train their people with what they need the person to know. Lastly, this is a safe question to start with; as the answer is simple to give … and perfectly sets up Question 2!

**Question 2**

*What do you like most about the job?*

Before founding my own company and becoming a professional speaker, author, and leadership trainer; I was a Mental Health Therapist for 19 years. I enjoyed the job, but more importantly ... I really enjoyed my clients. It was important for me to be aware that I may not have been my client's first therapist. Therefore, I started every new session by introducing myself and asking "Have you done therapy before?". Most of the time the answer was "Yes". Then I got to ask, "What did you like about it; if anything?" and "What didn't you like?". Most clients are never asked this question; as it's all about the therapist jumping in and sharing how they work. This question allows you to marry what they need with your style; creating an environment they look forward to coming to, evolving in, and paying for!

"What they like most about the job" also allows you (and the candidate) to hear what's most important to them! It may be flexibility, helping a mission grow, meeting new people, finishing tasks, etc. Now you know ... and so do they!

**Question 3**

*What frustrates you the most about the job ... Be honest!*

The "Be honest" at the end is important as it implies you know it's a sensitive question, you want "realness", and are curious. Interestingly enough, the most common answer I've heard was "Not knowing the expectations of my boss or my role".

This is a great time to discuss your view on leadership! I share my belief that leadership is a Two-Way Street ... It's my job to share the vision, expectations, and the few rules that propel us forward. It's also important we have a safe environment for you to ask questions, challenge ideas, and accompany any problem you may have with a suggested solution. We only move forward as a team!

The other side of the street involves employees being willing to ask questions, assertively seek clarification, and professionally challenge ideas with intent to impact the vision and/or process of things. For example, "I'm having a hard time understanding _____, can you help me grasp _____ so I can better explain it to my team to hit the goal?". Or, "I have an idea I believe will help with _____. I'd like to know what you like about it and if there's anything you'd fine-tune?". Perhaps, your candidate has a different answer to Question 3 … whatever the answer, it's true and powerful to them … be sure to listen and take it in!

## Question 4

*What's your dream … If it's this job, great! If it's not, great! What's your dream?*

I love asking this question, as most people's eyes widen when asked. Remember, the "What's your dream question" is a question most people are only asked as children and while in school. Sadly, as people enter the workforce, life, and raise families … this question fades and tends to disappear. I love this question because you may be the first person in a very long time or EVER to ask it! Your candidate may say this is their dream job, or one day want to start their own business, or they're in school to become a _____. Their answer will not only share more about them, but also shed light on ways you can possibly help.

A few years ago, I was presenting my Evolve & Lead Training Program for a company and all of their international leaders attended. The VP of the company introduced one of the leaders to me and said they were sad she would be leaving the company soon, but happy for her at the same time. The VP mentioned the woman would be leaving the company to open her own bakery and they've been helping to taste-test her goodies for over a year!!!! Do you think either party will forget the other? The leader that left will always kick back great people to that organization; as well as speak highly of the company when out in the world!

I recently interviewed an Executive Assistant and her answer to this question was she has a side-business, enjoys flexibility of working from home, and has a desire to do both jobs. I was honored to mail her my book and offer her my 1-on-1 Growth Sessions to enhance her leadership and work/life harmony! The better she is as a leader, professionally and personally, the more she will do for and with my vision and forgive the mistakes I will inherently make from time to time!

Whether it's related to your organization or beyond; how can you help your people with their dreams?

## Question 5
*How do you learn best?*

I've shared this in my book, 7 Ways to Lead, and in my Trainings for organizations. To simplify it … I believe there are four ways people learn best: Verbal, Written, Visual, or Hands-On. I'm more Hands-on; especially when it's a task I'm not going to do often. I need to do it, take notes, then be able to refer to my notes so I only have to ask questions one time. Lay these four options out for your candidates and see what they say. Their answer will tell you how to marry your teaching style with how they learn best. It can save you both mountains of frustration!

**Question 6**

*What are your Top 2 Professional Languages?*

I travel the most teaching and training my Leader's 7; The 7 Languages your people need, want, and benefit most hearing from leadership. Everyone likes all 7, but each person have their top one or two. Be Mindful ... when you decide to use this ... ask it every year; as people's Language can change as they evolve. For a deeper dive, feel free to read my 7 Ways to Lead. In the meantime, here are the 7 Languages that highly influence, impact, and motivate your people:

- Goodie-Time – Food: Pizza, Hoagies, Lunches, or simply ... chocolates in a bowl!
- Quality Minutes – Brief conversation that's not work-related with their boss!
- Recognition & Affirmation – Being recognized for their great work!
- Knowledge & Advancement – Wants to learn more and/or advance!
- Incentives – Enjoys earning bonuses, trips, winning company competitions, etc.!
- Flexibility – Work in a flexible manner or have ideas flexibly implemented!
- Respect – Have the necessary tools to succeed, email etiquette, tone of voice, ask don't tell.

Knowing our people's Language will allow you to consistently lead with their motivation in casual times and in those tough conversations you must be willing to have as a leader.

**Question 7**

*This is a Two-Way Street and you're interviewing me as much I'm interviewing you. Do you have any questions for me and what do you want to get out of working with us?*

Some candidates will have questions to get to know the company better, questions about their role, money, or hours. While others will have zero questions. Whether they have any or none; the important thing is ... you asked! Lastly, knowing what they want to get out of working with and for you is a gift ... allowing you to know where they want to go, what they want to know, and how you can be of impact in their professional journey! This is the opportunity to share what the job entails and what's most important to you about their job ... and can they do it!

I'm sure you have a few great questions of your own to ask or that you've been asked ... feel free to marry them with these and enhance not only your Leadership & Work/Life Harmony but also that of those new to your organization and team. Enjoy the journey!

> *"Knowing what your candidates want to get out of working with and for you is a gift ... allowing you to know where they want to go, what they want to know, and how you can be of impact in their professional journey!"*
> – Andre Young

# CHAPTER 5

# The Leader's 3!; The 3 Building Blocks of Leadership: Vision, Expectations, and Rules

You will find The Leader's 3 to be one of the most valuable assets you have when leading your people, your team, and your organization! They're the three building blocks focused on guiding and protecting your Mission Statement and enhancing the professional and personal leadership of those you lead! As a leader, you may know your company's mission statement; which tends to be too wordy, jargon-filled, vague, and let's be honest … just because you know it doesn't mean your people do! Remember, if your 13-year old can't say it and understand it … it's not simple enough!

The Leader's 3 is such a foundational building block you will see it referenced and built upon throughout this book! It's one of the key concepts in my Trainings and inevitably when I ask a leader their Leader's 3 … their eyes kind of roll back in their head a bit as they struggle to dig a bit deeper into their Vision, Expectations, and Rules. Remember, your Mission Statement is not the endpoint, rather a starting point to build upon! So what are the 3?

### Vision & Vision Factors

As the leader of a company, what's your Vision for your organization? If you're a leader of a team, what's your Vision for your team? When you don't know, how are your people supposed to? Having an answer to this question is the first step to becoming ELITE. Unfortunately, too many people stop here; as if having a vision is enough. If that were the case, everyone would have everything they ever wanted and be massively successful. Think about it … they're people rolling over right now scratching their backsides while having visions of being a millionaire. The last I checked, that doesn't put a million dollars in your bank account!

After Vision comes The Vision Factors … The 3-5 things that when done consistently, the Vision takes care of itself! I have a vision and it's written nicely on a whiteboard on my bathroom mirror, however I spend very little time looking at it because I'm too darn busy doing my Vision Factors … which, when DONE CONSISTENTLY, breed the success you desire!

So, what are the 3-5 things, that when done consistently … when YOUR PEOPLE and TEAMS do them consistently … the Vision will take care of itself?

Here's an example, my Vision is to be the best in the world in my space of Leadership & Work/Life Harmony; becoming wealthy (in Time & Money) with ideas I create, in a company I run. That's my Vision … sounds nice? But does nothing for me without my Vision Factors. So, what are they?

1. Create great content!

- I must create great videos, articles, books, speaking engagements, and trainings to offer to the world!
2. Network Appropriately!
   - My content isn't for everyone … so where are my people and how can I best engage and serve?
3. Passive Income Opportunities!
   - It's hard to get wealthy if you're not making money when you sleep.

When I consistently focus on these three things, my dream and vision come true! Knowing your Vision Factors will also make it easier to know what to say "Yes" and "No" to. As a leader, you will be bombarded with ideas from coworkers, employees, and outside entities. When an idea or partnership is offered and aligned with your Vision & Vision Factors … it's an easier "Yes". When an idea is not aligned with your Vision & Vision Factors … share your V & VF with the individual, explain their proposition is outside of your area of focus, and encourage them…on their own time … to fit their idea into your Vision & Vision Factors. When they can, great! If they can't … they may not like your "No", but they will respect your "No"!

**Expectations**

What are your Expectations for your People?

Your answer doesn't have to be long, and I implore you to keep it as short as possible. My answer is The 3 P's as you read in Chapter 3. Anyone I hire or partner with must be Positive, Passionate, and Productive!

## Rules

"Rules" sounds like such a harsh word! I'm oppositional by nature and never liked the word "Rules", however I understand you don't need many, but if you don't have any ... you won't be leading for very long! Rules are necessary in our lives as professionals, as a parent, in society, or chaos would ensue! Professionally, rules help to maintain a standard that everyone is aware of and accountable to.

### As a leader, what are your TOP 2-3 rules?

My Top 3 are simple:

1.  Be on time!
    - On-time means, please be where you said you were going to be, preferably 5 minutes before you said you'd be there. Being on time doesn't mean skirting into the parking lot at 7:00am, when you were scheduled for 7:00am. Please be ready to go, with a positive spirit, and a leader's mindset. Also, it's amazing the conversations and opportunities that can occur when you're a bit early ... Be Mindful!
2.  Email Issues
    - We go back and forth more than 3-4 times in email about the same thing ... let's get on a call and clean it up!
3.  Please accompany your problem with a suggested solution!
    - Many organizations and leaders tend to adopt this one! As a leader, this protects you from being Mr. or Ms. Fix-It all day long; enhancing the leadership skills of your people; their problem-solving skills, their willingness and ability to think like a leader, and brainstorm before coming to you with complaints and problems all day. Remember, you will most likely promote from

within … wouldn't it be great to promote someone with existing leadership skills?

- I always told my people … When you present an idea, one of three things will happen. One, the idea is so dang-on-good it blows my socks off and we have to go with it! Two, we may collaborate and work to fine-tune the idea; as they may not be aware of some bigger picture issues. Remember, your people don't sit in your seat or have access to your emails to know all that's going on. Three, we may not go with the idea because it's not aligned with the Vision & Vision Factors. When this is the case, encourage your people (on their own time) to better fit their idea into the V & VF and that you're available at this day and time … or … this day and time to discuss further. They now have to exhibit great leadership skills and show up at the time they selected!

I hope The Leader's 3 resonated with you and I encourage you to be clear and consistent in your 3 as you influence, impact, and protect your organization's culture!

*What was your Biggest Takeaway from The 3?*

*"You don't need many rules, but if you don't have any …*
*you won't be leading for very long … Be Mindful!!"*
– Andre Young

CHAPTER 6

# A Leader's Types; The 5 Types of Leaders ... The Pros & Concerns of Each!

There are many types of everything; different types of animals, people, foods, and ... Leaders! I'd like to share the 5 Types of Leaders; this is not to put leaders in a positive or negative category. Rather, an opportunity to celebrate ALL Leaders and a chance to examine the Pros & Concerns of your Type! It's important to note, a great leader will be all Five Types given the person or situation that requires it from them. However, we all have one or two types that really resonate with who we are at our core.

We must first define what we're discussing. A Leader is someone willing and capable of positively influencing people toward the mission of the team or organization. Is willing and capable of positively impacting others; leaving a lasting impression by words spoken, lessons taught, and actions taken. Is willing and capable of protecting others from themselves and their bad habits ...

and also protecting their people from their own bad habits and rough days. A Leader maintains high standards and expectations and effectively utilizes the individual superpower of those on their team to achieve success. Lastly, as a leader … you choose to show up daily with a smile, connecting, doing your best, and being your best! With that said, here are 5 Types of Leaders … Let's dive in!

**The Motivator**

This type of leader is high-energy, vocal, uplifting, and exuberant! They focus on the positives, the superpowers of others, and vocally push the team and lead toward the desired definition of success. You may know them as the emotional leader of a team … their energy, grit, and eagerness cannot be denied!

*The Pros*

I've had the opportunity to work for "The Motivator" and it was a great experience … as you feel like you have your own personal cheerleader! You feel believed in, supported, protected, and inspired. The pros of The Motivator are they are encouraging and forward-moving. They also tend to care very much for their people professionally and personally.

*The Concerns*

The truth is, not everyone feels like being motivated! Some employees, teammates, and co-workers are low-energy individuals who have never played on a team and cannot or will not understand the rah-rah approach. Others may see The Motivator's energy as fake, corny, and unnecessary.

It's important for "The Motivator" to hire well or recruit well … intentionally onboarding people with a good energy level, positivity, and enthusiasm … as well as a skill-set and knowledge base that will impact the team's leadership and work/life harmony and the organization! When your style as a Motivator isn't working ... it may be best to utilize The Leader's 7 we explored in Chapter 4. Knowing how to speak a different language, the desired language of your people never hurts!

When you work for "The Motivator" compliment them on their passion. I'm a motivator by nature and one of the best compliments I receive is, "You're so passionate about what you do". It inevitably brings a smile to my face ... and smiles tend to open ears ... Be Mindful!

## The Example

This is the leader that quietly leads by example. They DO all of the right things, but in a much more quiet manner than The Motivator. If you were a fly on the wall ... all you would see is this leader doing the "right things" in the "right way" all day long!

### The Pros

"The Example" sets the bar for how to get things done! Progress is steady, they're self-motivated, and self-starters.

### The Concerns

Although "The Example" gets things done and does things the right way; this leader may lack the winning people skills to lead a team. This doesn't mean they aren't nice or care about people ... they simply may struggle with effectively connecting with the different types of individuals on their team or throughout the organization. As "The Example" when you choose to know and understand what each of your people desires to get out of working at the job or on the team, being willing to connect, and somewhat speak the desired language of others to marry what you want with what they need ... connection is created ... and connection matters!

Remember, leadership is a two-way street. When you work for "The Example", schedule time to ask questions and share ideas to get a better grasp on things. The Example tends to be more than willing to help, but due to having their head down and getting things done; they are not likely to step forward to initiate.

**The Connector**

This is the leader that actively connects with their people and their team. They know their people's stories, their kids' names, their lives professionally and personally. You may see this leader or employee floating through the office talking with everyone, engaging in chit-chat, having serious conversations, or emotionally helping their people through tough times.

It may appear this leader is not focused on their work or may be behind in their work because they are so social. However, because they are a leader ... they are on top of their responsibilities and enhancing the quality of the team as well.

*The Pros*

"The Connector" exhibits powerful understanding, empathy, and care for those around them and especially those on their team. They tend to be eager, responsible, and possess powerful people skills. Plus, their people like and enjoy them!

*The Concerns*

Although "The Connector" possesses great people skills they may struggle to actually bring a team together; influencing progess as a team. It may seem odd they can be so engaging 1-on-1, but struggle to motivate the group. A new "Connector Leader" may often want to be one of the guys … instead of the leader.

This leads into concern number two; because "The Connector" may be too emotionally invested or enjoys being one of the team … it may be difficult for them to have those dreaded tough conversations with their employees. "The Connector" is not likely to change their personality … and that's a good thing … however, being able and willing to use The World's Best Preface Statement will be useful for their leadership. It sounds like, "It's wonderful to have you on the team and I enjoy leading, guiding, and supporting. However, at some point, I may have to say something that's hard for you to hear or have questions to ask … and I wouldn't be doing my job if I didn't. Is that going to be OK?".

Whether the tough conversation comes two days from now or two years from now … when it's time for "The Connector" to have the tough conversation, it will be easier and can sound like, "Remember the time I said I might have to say something that's hard to hear or have questions to ask? Ready? Now, you hit them with it, discuss the issue, and work to develop a plan of action to best move forward. This process will allow "The Connector" to maintain their personality while being a leader the team and organization needs.

When you work for "The Connector" ask them about their day, their weekend, their plans for the holiday, etc. Follow-Up to see how things are going for them and don't forget to thank them from time to time for always maintaining interest in you.

**The Visionary**
This Leader is mostly bigger-picture, big ideas, and grand vision for the future of the organization! They stand on the mountain top, see farther, and think bigger. Many people may not see

or understand their vision, but "Visionaries" propel companies forward by positively pushing the envelope and the skills of their people. Ask Blockbuster Video if they wish they'd listened to their Visionaries!

*The Pros*

"The Visionary" is focused on bigger ideas, is forward-thinking, and encourages those around them to think bigger. They make people and the things they're working on better.

*The Concerns*

Because "The Visionary" is focused on bigger things they tend to dislike, be unorganized with, unfamiliar with, or lack understanding of the numerous little things it takes to make the big thing a reality. This leader may struggle with empathy related to the countless hours, demands, restarts, and burn-out of their people.

The vision will most likely be achieved, but at what cost! The saddest thing is when Inspired & Motivated employees burn-out and quit ... or burn-out and stay. Be mindful to observe and care for your people and team as they bring your BIG Ideas to life!

When you work for "The Visionary" it tends to be best to start with the Big Idea, have a solution ready for how you plan to make it happen, and be prepared to answer questions as asked.

**The Intense**

This leader is gruff, blunt, and abrupt in their approach. They are not interested in making friends, connecting, motivating, or setting an example. "The Intense is focused on the task and getting it done right, on time, and within the numbers projected. It may seem this leader is no fun however, they get results. "The Intense" is not mean to others; rather a bit serious. When they enter the room, you may see people straighten up, decide to look busy, and get more done than they would if "The Intense" was not there.

### The Pros

"The Intense" is dependable, a thinker, and consistent. Although they are not buddy-buddy and people may struggle on how to approach them ... they are available, willing, and ready; just be sure to get to the point quickly ... and be a ready and willing participant in the vision.

### The Concerns

"The Intense" can be so focused on task completion, numbers, and not having to answer questions from their superiors ... they may struggle with the leadership ability to control the ebb & flow of the team, the office, or the organization. Leaders never drop their standards and expectations, but leaders also understand people can only operate at maximum go-time for so long. You must know when your people or team need a break, some relief, something different, something fun ... and also know when and how to retighten the reigns to get back to work!

Also, it helps when "The Intense" knows they are intense. Most people can alter their behaviors, but you are who you are at your core! Some leaders are intense by nature, while others may feel they need to be "Intense" to gain ... and keep ... the respect of their team. I hear this a lot from new leaders coming into an existing team or women working in male-dominated industries.

When "The Intense" can hire or promote "A Motivator" or "A Connector" to be their right-hand person ... an awesome buffer is created to lessen the blow of "The Intense" and positively benefit the team and organization in the process. This DOES NOT give "The Intense" the green light to become MORE INTENSE. However, it provides an opportunity to evolve and learn new skills!

Again, when your style as "The Intense" isn't working … it may be best to utilize The Leader's 7 we explored in Chapter 4. Knowing how to speak a different language … the desired professional language of your people never hurts!

When you work for the intense, schedule time to ask questions and share ideas. Ask for clarification to help you better understand concepts or processes; allowing you to best share necessary information with your team. Share ideas; having essential information to enhance your point and start with, "I have an idea I believe will help with _____. It'd be great to hear what you like about it and anything you'd fine-tune". This flow and mix of introduction and questioning helps to remove your ego and invite theirs in … I call it, A Leader's Idea!

This is The 5 Types of Leaders! Which are your Top 2? Remember, great leaders are all five, given the person or situation that requires it of them … and now you know the Pros & Concerns of each and what to do when you work for a certain type. Enjoy!

*"A great leader can be all Five Types of Leaders given the person or situation that requires it from them … Be Mindful"*
– Andre Young

# CHAPTER 7

# A Leader's Caution; The 5 Types of Managers!

I'd like to preface this chapter by saying this is no knock on anyone with the title of Manager. You've earned your way up the ladder and congrats on your success! I'd like to share my definition of a Leader vs. a Manager; a leader exudes and exhibits the definition of leadership you read in Chapter 2. A Manager may give out orders, but lacks the power of connection or has yet to develop the leadership skills of positive influence, impact, protection, and on-the-spot decision making. When first promoted to leadership positions, we all become Managers before we know how to lead … it's par for the course on your journey to evolving as a leader!

It helps to understand most promotions are given to employees that did one thing really well. You sold a million dollars' worth of product … you're now the Sales Manager! It doesn't mean you know how to lead; it simply means you know how to sell a million dollars' worth of product your way. You'll most likely want to teach that way and those that don't succeed, by your definition, become a thorn in your side.

Here are the 5 Types of Managers many people become after a promotion, what to beware, and what to do!

### The Ego

This was me many years ago. I was promoted to lead a team of therapists; I was working in the field, completed my Master's Degree, had the knowledge and skillset to provide therapy, was promoted to a leadership position, and now I'm supervising my ex-coworkers and friends. Sound familiar?

The problem was, I knew how to do therapy, but I didn't know how to lead! Therefore, my ego was based on my knowledge of therapy (for you, it may be the knowledge of your product or years worked). I wanted everyone to know what I knew, operate the way I operated, and was actively working to create a bunch of Mini-Me's.

Although I provided recognition & affirmation and passed on knowledge, my ego didn't allow me to acknowledge, respect, and effectively utilize each person's superpowers on my team. I had the world's best Case Manager on my team, the world's best Crisis Manager, an incredible Therapist, and the world's largest Classroom De-Escalator; standing 6'5 and 360lbs! A manager … especially a manager with an ego wants to create mini-me's. A Leader can see the value and superpower of his people individually and collectively, put them in the right seats, and thrive no matter the conditions … Be Mindful!

### The Climber

This is the manager focused on climbing the ladder. The titles, promotions, raises, and the rise to the top is their everything. The positive is … they are eager, motivated, and inspired. The negative is, it's all about them! This is the manager you're scared will steal your idea, take all the credit, or throw you under the bus to protect themselves or get ahead.

If you are working under a Climber, following up on conversations via email may be a great idea. Black & White doesn't lie! If you are a Climber, remember your positive is your ambition. Use that energy to ambitiously connect with your team. First, understand the vision of the organization, the vision factors, the expectations, and rules. Next, be sure your team is aware … you'd be surprised how many employees don't know the bigger picture of the company; leading to constant questioning, complaining, gossiping, and low effort level.

It's also imperative to give credit to your team and the specific individuals on your team … do this in groups, in private, and in emails to be sure credit is going where it needs to. Leaders accept all of the blame in bad times and none of the credit in the good times! When your team is successful … people know who the leader is! Your final step is getting to know your people:

- Why are they here working for the organization?
- What do they want to get out of the experience?
- How do you marry their wants/aspirations to the organization's vision of success; creating win-wins for you, them, and the company!

**The Abuser**

This is the person promoted to a position of power and is abusive and abrasive. The reasons can vary. Perhaps they've felt powerless throughout their lives and now have a badge of power they feel gives them the right to be sharp, demanding, and aggressive. Perhaps they struggle to connect with people and reading social cues is not their strong point. Perhaps, they're nervous and a rough approach is how they handle stressful situations. Perhaps they're stressed and burnt-out. There are many more possibilities, but none make it ok to be verbally, emotionally, or physically abusive to your staff. Vulgar comments, rude jokes, name-calling, close-proximity intimidation, sexual advances, threats, etc. must not be tolerated by organizations, leaders, or employees.

If you are an employee in a situation like this, please report it immediately! You can be in a better situation, whether in your company or another ... the leaders in your organization need to know! Perhaps they are unaware ... or perhaps they are, have had conversations with The Abuser, and you letting them know is the final straw.

If you are The Abuser, my feedback is simple ... STOP! When you don't know what to say, speak The Leader's 7; the 7 Languages your people need, want, and benefit most hearing from leadership.

**The Friend**

It can be difficult to be promoted to Manager and now manage your friends. You may also have a friendly personality and like being in the weeds with your team. The positive is your people like you and know you care about them. The potential setback is that it may be difficult for you to have the tough conversation when necessary. As I mentioned before, The World's Best Preface Statement can help!

"I'm excited about the new position and looking forward to working with you/everyone. I know this change is awkward; we're going to have some great wins and will be sure to celebrate them. We will also have some rough times and I may have to say something that's hard for you to hear or question things from time to time, but I wouldn't be doing my job if I didn't. Is that going to be ok?". 99% of the people nod their heads and say "Yes". The person that says "No" ... beware! It may also be helpful to ask, "When I have to ask questions or say something hard for you to hear, how do you prefer I come to you about it?". See what they say and marry it with your style. This may prove to be a big help as you begin your leadership journey with former co-workers and even friends who may be happy for your success ... or not so much!

At some point, 6 minutes from now or 6 months from now ... an employee will make a mistake and the conversation can sound like ... "Hi _____. Do you have a second? Remember when I said I may have to say something that's hard for you to hear or question some things? Ready? You will watch them physically and emotionally brace for impact ... some with a smile, a nod, a deep breath, or even a giggle. For more, check out the full Leader's 7 in my previous book, 7 Ways to Lead!

**The Incompetent**

This is the person promoted to leadership or transferred to a new team without having the knowledge or skill set for the job. Perhaps they were great where they were, but it's significantly different in the new position. The mistakes of The Incompetent can cause significant financial loss, employee loss, decreased morale, and the dissolution of a team.

If you are working under The Incompetent you have a choice:

1. Suffer under their management, engage in the gossip, and become a cog in the system as morale plummets
2. Engage with the Manager, offer support, understanding, and ask what they need most from you right now. Remember, managers are people too ... and it's most likely they're going through an array of thoughts and feelings; including

anxiety, frustration, excitement, and an eagerness to prove themselves.

If you are The Incompetent ... I don't use this word to be rude. It simply means you are unaware and do not know what you need to know to be successful in the current position you occupy. So, be sure you know the expectations the organization has for you, know your strengths to help get the job done, know your weak spots (you may not know immediately, but situations will arise as a Manager that will show you), admit what you don't know, select leaders within your team; revealing your situation and solicit their advice as you work to get more acclimated.

It always amazed me how many employees believe managers either know it all or should know it all. What a way to break the mold as a manager, by admitting you don't and creating a Right-Hand Person until you can walk on your own!

You now know the 5 pitfalls suffered by those managing before they evolve into leaders. You have a choice ... Manage or Lead. Enjoy your evolution!

*"Leaders accept all the blame in bad times and none of the credit in the good times! When your team is successful ... people know who the leader is!"*
– Andre Young

# CHAPTER 8

# A Leader's Team; Utilizing Your 5 Rockstars!

I'll preface this by stating, EVERYONE within your organization and Team is and can be a Rockstar! You probably don't believe me, and that's OK! At the core, I believe most people want to be good at their job and have good intentions ... however, many companies and leaders get trapped attempting to MOTIVATE their employees, which can be dangerous! Can you imagine being the coach of a sports team and having to always motivate your players to practice and play games ... it would be exhausting for you, eat away at your love for the job, and eventually negatively impact your Leadership & Work/Life Harmony ... and theirs!

As you've already read, my rule when building a team is ... The 3 P's. Are the people you're bringing in Positive, Passionate, and Productive? When this is the case, everyone is a Rockstar and ready to find the seat within the organization that fits them best! Now, this may not be the case for you, as you may have inherited a team. They may have been promoted, transferred, new to a company, or due to an employee shortage, the organization simply hired a bunch of bodies. The good news is, everyone can be a Rockstar, and whether you've gotten to hand-pick your team or you inherited one … there are 5 Key Types of Team Members to focus on. So, who are they and how do you it?

### The Seller!

I'll define "Power" as the ability to influence. The scary thing is, power and influence can go one of two ways … for the better or for the worse … and the person with the power may not always be you! It sounds odd; you're the boss, the one with the title, but you may quickly find there may be one or a few employees underneath your title that the team and the front-line listen to more and take their cues from.

I've been on both sides, being the Positive Seller and The Destructive Seller. Let's start with destructive … many years ago, as a Mental Health Therapist, I entered a facility in year two of its inception and had a ball starting something from scratch. Professionally, it was a great time in my life and it lasted for about 15 years. Looking back, I'm grateful to have had the experience and lucky it lasted as long as it did; but all great things must come to an end!

With the change of CEO, a slew of administrative changes, policy changes, and a new direct boss … all things came crashing down; including my morale, leadership, positivity, passion, and production! However, I was still "The Seller," and people were buying what I was selling; that the new boss was incompetent, was not fit for the job, what I would do instead, and that the system was broken. I spouted all this with no suggested plan of action or willingness to be a part of the solution! As a leader, please know the grouches on your team are not only miserable ... they also recruit! As a person of my standing back then ... more co-workers, employees, and supervisors listened to me than my boss; however, I was no longer fit to wield that type of power; and eventually, the company agreed as well!

Years later, I had the privilege of being "The Positive Seller". I accepted a full-time sales position; while at the same time doing my business full-time and getting off the ground. I had twelve staff and was in a much better place professionally, personally, and in my leadership. It was important for me to give the company that hired me the same respect and effort I wanted from my employees. Although I was not in a position of leadership, I chose to show up daily with a smile, willing to do my best, be my best, speak my best, learn, and encourage (Personal Leadership). Some followed, some knew where to go when times were hard, and the Negative Nicks and Nancys knew not to bring gossip my way!

In both accounts as a leader, whether you have The Positive or The Destructive Seller ... it may enhance your leadership to acknowledge their skillset and role, and rather than be intimidated by it ... utilize it to positively impact the team. When I was the "Destructive Seller", it would have meant the world to me for my new boss to say, "I know I'm new here and you seem to have the lay of the land, how things work, and who to go to. I'd like to lean on you for a while with some big and small things. I have a vision and your feedback would be helpful until I can get my bearings. I don't promise we will always see eye-to-eye or that I can use everything you share, but I'll be sure to give a real explanation and the bigger picture. Thank You for everything you've done before I got here and for all we'll accomplish moving forward!". Feel free to make this your own. The truth is, some will love this and see you as open, sincere, and willing. Others may see you as weak and you "should" know all the answers due to taking their promotion, earing more money, or having the leadership title. The point is to acknowledge their role, their power, and the possibility to make an impact!

Lastly, The Seller is the team member that may help to sell tough ideas to co-works and front-line employees. As a leader, it's your job to lead ... however a little help and partnerships can go a long way in smoothing rough edges in a tumultuous work environment! Share the news with The Seller beforehand or after the team meetings; be sure to answer their questions and share the benefits for the employee, the team, and the organization. When The Seller has a better understanding of "The Why" and "The How" it will arm them with the necessary information needed when they are inevitably bombarded with gripes and complaints from coworkers!

**The Personality!**

This is the team member with the BIG personality! They light up a room when they walk in, everyone knows them, they're positive, engages with everyone, and the cherry on top ... they're great at their job! What a wonderful person to be the face of your organization when out in public!

Years ago, my business did a lot of work on college campuses, impacting young men and women. There were two interns I labeled, The Personality! They were both motivated, inspiring, charismatic, and engaging ... perfect to wear the You Evolving Now tee shirts around campus to network and recruit. The difference ... one intern was the BIG Personality and positive all the time; while the other was a BIG Personality and had two-faces. I observed it happen one day as I was on campus. While he was officially on the clock ... he was inspiring, pleasant, and positive. AS SOON AS

THE EVENT WAS OVER ... BAM ... a totally different person; vulgar language and inappropriate conversations! Be mindful, before making your "Personality" the face of your mission, vision, or organization ... be sure they are that way consistently!

When I was working in the sales position, I faced a dilemma ... I wanted to be the face of my own company and also wanted to make as much money as possible at the sales job. I was scheduled to attend a networking event and didn't want to be the guy handing out two different business cards. I chose my business! However, what an impact it would have been for my sales and the company I worked for me to be the face of the store out in the world! Who is "The Personality" on your team? Are they consistently positive, passionate, and productive? How can a win-win be created; having them represent your brand and vision out in the world, networking, and/or social media?

**The Closer!**

The Closer is the team member you trust to get things done! When the stuff hits the fan, you have that important project due, that high profile client/customer needs tending to ... this is the team member you trust to take it across the finish line. I often talk about the word protection as a lost word when it comes to leadership ... Protecting our people from themselves and their bad habits with boundaries and rules, protecting our time as leaders, and protecting our people from us. "The Closer" requires your protection; as they are known for getting stuff done ... and also known by everyone else for the same thing! Therefore, you think he/she has only their work and the favors you've asked them to do on their list; not knowing everyone else in the office has asked them to do three things as well. Compound this day after day, week after week, month after month, year after year, decade after decade ... how do you think they're supposed to feel about their job, their coworkers, and YOU?

Protect and care for your "Closers" by:

- Knowing what they want to get out of working for you and the organization
- What's their vision professionally
- What are their dreams and how can you and the organization help
- Having regularly scheduled 1-on-1 Meetings with a focus on knowing their "List" and how to best help them prioritize, delegate, or subtract

**The Peacekeeper!**

This may be a hard team member to identify; as a lot of their actions and interactions will happen away for you. Coworkers are getting into verbal spats ... they're the ones to settle things down. The Peacekeeper is the quiet and subtle voice of reason on the floor, on the job, over the call, or emails. They may be the gentle greeting or smile needed by a new employee or a stressed employee. Years ago, I was providing ongoing Leadership Training at an organization and had the honor of meeting with so many of their wonderful employees. While meeting with staff, one employee's name kept coming up as a person that was pleasant, a hard worker, and most importantly a nice and a soft-spot for struggling and socially isolated employees. Her name came up so much that I felt like I was meeting Mother Teresa when she walked through the door ... and I was honored to shake her hand!

As a leader, my advice is to start asking your staff periodically ... who is the Peacekeeper here? When you're having a bad day or feel alone at work, who do you turn to? Who would you say is the nicest, listens the best, gives the best advice? There must be a way to reward someone so valuable to your team, the organization, and for your client/customer base!

**Everyone!**

As I stated initially, everyone within your organization and team is a Rockstar! They may not be currently exhibiting Rockstar interactions or production; however, I believe everyone has Rockstar potential. Did they have it starting with your organization and it fizzled due to poor leadership practices? Did it fizzle due to being burnt-out or bored-out? Did you simply hire a body and that's what you got ... a passionless breathing body? In either case, they show up every day for a reason ... perhaps they want to learn more about the job, want to move up, the job is a steppingstone, or they simply need that paycheck once every two weeks. Whatever their "Why" ... find out what it is, how to help, set or reset some high expectations and high standards, and start a new day and new culture!

> *"As a leader, please know the grouches on your team are not only miserable ... they also recruit ... Be Mindful!"*
> – Andre Young

# CHAPTER 9

## A Leader's 1-on-1 Meetings; The "Need" and The "How"!

Throughout this book, I'll refer to A Leader's 1-on-1 Meetings often; as it's one of the most leadership enhancing tools you'll have in your toolbox. However, as critical as this tool is, it's also the easiest tool to ignore as the 1-on-1 Meeting is the most canceled and rescheduled meeting across all organizations!

Many leaders and organizations recognize the value and importance of 1-on-1's. Still, they often have them because it was deemed necessary by company policy ... leading to subpar meetings with their managers spouting projected metrics solely focused on the benefit of the organization. Or, the 1-on-1's are scheduled, but often canceled or rescheduled due to being "Busy" ... as if "Busy" will never dissipate! Especially with the amount increased remote and hybrid work ... leadership, connection, and motivation are more important than ever. So, what to do and how to do it?

It first makes sense to define what a 1-on1 Meeting is. Let's define it as a meeting between a leader and employee to connect, understand, grow, and improve; to positively impact the Leadership and Work/Life Harmony of the leader, the employee, the team, and the organization as a whole!

I once worked for a company that initiated 1-on-1 Meetings. My manager came to us as a team and revealed the 1-on-1's would begin the following week; with the focus to help each Sales Person meet their desired goals and improve their craft. I thought, "I'm all in!". I'm always eager to DO and BE better ... and as a former athlete, the coaching aspect was very attractive. The day came and my Manager approached me for our meeting. Sadly to say, it was nothing like how I thought it'd be; rather an awful rendition of an Annual Review on a weekly basis. He shared my sales numbers with me, told me areas he felt I could improve ... or rather the areas the organization desired more sales in, gave me metrics to hit ... as if I hit them; the numbers wouldn't go up, and this type of meeting went on for weeks.

I remember leaving those meetings irritated and frustrated ... very much the opposite of upbeat, encouraged, and ready! Not only did I exit those 1-on-1's in that manner; I watched almost every one of my coworkers walk out of their meetings with shoulders slumped and seeming uninspired. In the months to come the 1-on-1's disappeared as quickly as they were introduced ... sound familiar? I very much believe in the power and impact of 1-on-1 Meetings, but done in a different way!

Let's start by introducing 1-on-1 Meetings to your team, but also sharing what the flow of the meeting will be. This may help reduce anxiety ... for you and for them! The more everyone knows what to expect; the better the meeting! The more they like the meeting, the more they'll share the positivity of the 1-on-1 amongst coworkers … and that's powerful!

The other big part is to schedule the meetings with your people. I know, you're "Busy" and I fully understand. However, I'm going to respectfully say "So what!". You're busy, they're busy, everyone's busy, and no one is ever going to be less busy. This is a meeting that works to enhance your reputation as a leader and enhance your work/life harmony for you and your people … Therefore, it's an important enough meeting to schedule! Also, be sure it's in your calendar and theirs; with the expectation it's important and not to be missed.

I often suggest the 1-on-1's be done monthly and scheduled three months out. The alternative is being your daily version of "busy", forgetting about the meetings, then attempting to squeeze them in as you pop into your people's office door, cubicle, or email to suddenly ask if they have time for a 1-on-1 with you … as if they have the power to say no. Then off you go to a sudden, rushed, and awful meeting. No Thank You! It also proves to be a great idea to put a timeframe on the meeting … 20 minutes. I've done it in 7 minutes … I've done it in 45 minutes. When you end early, great! If you go over a bit, great! If you're busy and the 20 minutes is just right amount of time, great! The point is, having a time frame will keep you on schedule and the business of your day flowing!

Now it's time to share the bullet points of the 1-on-1 Meeting; allowing you and your employee to reap the full leadership benefits:

**The P.O.W.**

Start each of your meetings with the P.O.W., The Positive of the Week! I start all my bigger trainings this way and it's truly a powerful way to start with a group or individual; allowing you to get positive and human-to-human very quickly!

The two key points are:

1. You must announce what the P.O.W. is … "We're always going to start our 1-on-1's with the Positive of the Week. As leaders, we really want to know our people and how to best celebrate them! What's been your positive of the past week; I'll go first to give you some time to think."

2. As a leader, you MUST go first … at least the first time! Afterward, simply ask their P.O.W. and enjoy their answer … whatever it may be.

It's necessary you go first … for two big reasons. Many employees live their lives and, like most people; focused on the negative or simply droning through the day. This positive question has not been asked to them in a long time or ever … so it knocks them on their heels a bit. If you expect them to go first you may hear crickets or something they think you want to hear. Two, when you go first … you give them time to think and also provide an example of how to answer!

You can share something about your kids, their sports, your vacation, your partner, work … it doesn't matter as long as it's true and genuine to you! As a leader, I encourage you to share something personal and something professional. After you share and offer them an opportunity; please give them the option to do either professional, personal, or both … whichever they're comfortable with. Not every employee likes mixing home and work.

In doing the P.O.W., it always amazes me the things people share. I've heard people have become grandparents, their son got all A's, their daughter stopped getting bullied in school, their son hit the game-winning shot, they met metrics or closed a big deal, and so much more! While few may say ... "I'm on the right side of the dirt". Although a seemingly bleak outlook ... it's a start and truly may be their only positive given their current life circumstances. NEVER minimize a positive shared and ALWAYS thank them for sharing!

What happens as you do the P.O.W. every time, you'll find that people become prepared for you. They know their 1-on-1 is coming, they know you're going to ask their P.O.W., so they prepare thinking of an answer the night before or the morning of. How about that for a positive impact and improvement in mindset amongst your team and organization! Sharing the P.O.W. not only allows you both to get human-to-human ... it also gives you something to speak about in casual times in the office or on remote calls; increasing connection and cohesiveness!

**Get Out of It**

This is a simple, yet powerful next question ... ask your attendee, "What would you like to get out of our meeting today?

This question makes the meeting about them and makes you keenly aware of what's important to them professionally and personally ... and why? When they have an answer, delve into their "why" and their proposed solution of how to make it happen. Their response meshed with your vision and expectations allow you to effectively lead and impact them ... and the organization!

When they don't have an answer ... that's OK too! Some of your employees are "Inspired & Motivated", but are unaware of ideas or questions to ask. Some are "Steady Streams" and fine right where they are; therefore may not have an answer. While others may be "Grouches" and could care less about the job, the meeting, or even you. When your employee doesn't have an answer, it's ok to move on and focus on what you, the team, or the organization needs most from them right now.

## Mesh Goals

It's time to mesh what the employee desires to get out of the meeting with what you and the organization need most for them right now. This can prove to be an excellent marriage; creating win-wins for you and them!

It's also a perfect time to ask what your employee is currently working on, what they are proud of, anything they're struggling with, and what they need help with. I refer to this as "A Leader's List". Sometimes we do a poor job as leaders being aware of our people's list ... we'll get more into that later in the book. One of the saddest things is when an "Inspired & Motivated" employee burns-out because their list is too long or bores-out because their list is too short! Either is bad for you, them, and the company.

1. It's helpful to know your employee's top two professional languages from my Leader's 7 ... are they Goodie-Time (like treats, coffee, etc.), Quality Minutes, Recognition & Affirmation, Knowledge & Advancement, Incentives, Flexibility, or Respect. Once you know.. speak it!

2. Remember I shared the importance of knowing your people's dreams? What a great time to ask about it and how it's going!

## Plan

Now that you know what your employee wants to get out of the meeting and you've meshed goals ... it's time to develop a plan!

Be sure to recap the plan post-meeting in a work email. I know it's one more thing to do; however, an undocumented meeting never happened! This protects you as a leader that you had the conversation, shared the bullet points of the 1-on-1, and everything that was agreed upon. Everyone you're leading on this professional journey may not finish with you … and when that time comes, you may need proper documentation … Be Mindful!

### Biggest Takeaway

To properly conclude your 1-on-1 Meeting ask your employee "What was your biggest takeaway of our meeting today?".

Asking this question makes whatever they say more real and impactful to them; than whatever you would've shared. Their answer may surprise you; as what you thought was great is entirely different from what they got out of the meeting. The point is, they get to walk out of their Meeting or close their laptop feeling great and fulfilled … and it will show on their face and in their body language. Remember when I shared seeing my coworkers walk out of their meeting with slumped shoulders and a scowl; you're people are always watching … Be Mindful!

Asking "What was your biggest takeaway from our meeting today?" sends your people out in a way that positively impacts your team. It will also allow one of the best conversations about your leadership to occur … that you will rarely get to hear. When Sally asks Bob if he's had his 1-on-1 yet and Bob says, "No, I don't want to; it's going to be stupid!" … Sally gets to say, "No, you're really going to like it. Mine was great!" … and that's priceless!

Lastly, it's important to note; as excited as you are to start your 1-on-1's … the impact is rarely felt in the first meeting. Moreso over time (3-4 regularly scheduled 1-on-1's) as they begin to build upon one another. Remember, this is already old information to you … it's brand new to your people and may take them a bit a time to adjust to the new you and new way!

*"A 1-on-1 Meeting is a meeting between a leader and employee to connect, understand, grow, and improve; to positively impact the leadership and work/life harmony of each attendee and the organization as a whole!"*

– Andre Young

# CHAPTER 10

## A Leader's Circle; Leading with other Leaders!

When most people hear the word "Leader", they may visualize one person leading a group; whether at a company, a sport, the military, etc. It's quite common to think of a leader leading alone. However, this is rarely the case! Leaders within organizations often have other leaders at their level (their coworkers) and bosses they report to: CEOs report to a Board, Senior Executives report to the CEO, Middle-Management report to Senior Leadership, Head Coaches to General Managers and Owners, and in your personal life ... although you're a leader ... you may have a significant other. The fact is, leaders are on a team too ... and it's not always pretty! Leaders can disagree on a plethora of things: what's most important at the moment, personality clashes, ego of whose job or department works the hardest and is most important, how to best follow through with plans, and more! Sound familiar? So, what to do?

**Remember The Vision & Vision Factors!**

I've mentioned The Leader's 3 many times and it's for a reason ... It will prove to be the staple for your leadership and reputation as a leader, team, and organization; allowing you to know what to say "Yes" and "No" to.

When leaders gather to review the organization's current standing and how to best proceed ... be sure "The Vision" is the guiding star! Once everyone is clear on the overriding Vision of the organization ... what's the Vision each leader has for their team? This is important to know; as everyone's vision doesn't have to match the Mission Statement or BIG Vision previously shared, however it must align!

Developing and knowing the Vision & Vision Factors for your team ... as well as the other teams that exist outside of your department, will be the first step in celebrating the good times and working through the frustrating times with other leaders!

**Listening**

It sounds simple but proves to be one of the hardest things when you're frustrated and determined to make your point to other leaders within the organization. Inevitably, there will come a time when you will disagree with another leader and you'll be presented with a choice to either bring your ego or your ears to the battle. When you lead with your ego and it wins ... you're more likely to attempt to dominate that way again, and again, and again. When you decide to ask and listen first ... you may find they have several points you agree with; allowing a mutual starting point. I'm not promising sunshine and rainbows ... simply something you, as a leader, can positively acknowledge about their perspective!

Here's a question to ask, "I can see you believe strongly in this, can you tell me/us more about it and what's the upside?". Allow them to share, actively listen, take notes if necessary (some people feel as though they are being heard when notes are taken), and later ask questions you may have regarding their idea's functionality within the bigger picture. Remember, very few ideas are perfect … the goal is to start and evolve it as you go!

**Most Important**

As a leader, you have concerns and ideas, other leaders have concerns and ideas, and the team has concerns and ideas. EVERY-THING cannot be done right now and right away! "Most Important" means … which are the 1,2, or 3 that are MOST IMPORT-ANT, why, and do they address the Vision & Vision Factors? When you consistently focus on the 1,2, or 3 MOST IMPORTANT … some of the other problems on the list will dissipate because they're byproducts of something bigger you're now addressing. For example … In my business, networking is one of my Vision Factors. However, my success was creating a new "Busy" for me and taking the necessary time away from networking. Addressing this concern became "Most Important"; leading me to bring in the right person and system to take away the burdens of traditional networking and evolving my process via Social Media.

**Sacrifice**

This is simple, yet painful. When you're on a team … you will not always get your way! Even when you have the most excellent idea of all time; due to timing, it may not be "The Most Import-ant" due to other pressing concerns. As a leader, you may have to sacrifice and cheer someone else's win … as your idea is great, but does not address the immediate pain of the team, organization, or customer!

## Follow Through

Both my sons play sports; whether it's shooting a jump shot or throwing a pass … the outcome is always better with the proper motion and full follow through! The same goes for our professional leadership. When that meeting adjourns … CONSISTENTLY do the plan and freakin follow through!

It starts with informing, educating, possibly training, encouraging your team or yourself, and following through until the plan is complete! Too many people let "Busy" beat them … leaving the meeting and allowing the duties, professional fires, emails, etc. to gut-punch them; knocking out the possibility of Follow Through. I'm sure you've had the experience of meeting after meeting about the same thing … and months later nothing has happened! Put "Follow Through Tasks" into your calendar; allowing you to win the day, support your leadership peers, and enhance your leadership. Remember, your idea may be selected next as "Most Important" and you're going to want the follow-through of other leaders!

> *"There will come a time when you will disagree with another leader on your team and you'll be presented with a choice to either bring your ego or your ears to the battle"*
> – Andre Young

# CHAPTER 11

# A Leader's 5 Types of Clients ... and what they need most from you!

W hether you're in a leadership position, an employee, or an entrepreneur ... you care for, serve, and lead your clients/ customers! Clients are what make your business matter; without clients you simply have a great idea, a vision, passion, and dream ... Clients make it count! Since clients are of utmost importance, let's define what they are and who they are. I define clients as people or organizations you do ONGOING business with. As a leader, you or your organization will be involved in fulfilling your clients' dreams; therefore, it makes sense to know what type of client you're working with and what they need most out of the experience. I've found there are 5 Types of Clients, so who are they and what do they need most from you?

**The Ghost**

The Ghost is the client that disappears after the contract is signed. Let's back up ... you or your organization have courted the client and earned the opportunity to be of value and impact and afterward, the client becomes a ghost and you don't hear from them or see them unless you reach out. This can happen for several reasons: perhaps they trust you and don't want to be involved in the process or they've gotten busy with other things such as personal issues, a promotion, the list can go on!

The positive is you have free reign to do what you want and be of impact without interruption, interference, and no micro-managing! For some, this feeling of autonomy is great; allowing you to lead your way.

The negative is, contracts don't last forever and there will be a time to reconvene and decide if you and your organization will continue as is, add more services, different services, or part ways. Best case scenario ... you nailed it with everything you've provided, met all expectations, and solved problems they didn't even know existed. This could happen, but most likely ... when the contract is up, the Ghost will simply fade away and continue to ghost your attempts to resign their business; leaving you dazed and confused. You may decide to email The Ghost asking what the issue was and what you could have done differently. In my experience, this is to no avail as they rarely get back to you with an answer ... and as a leader, this is your fault! Allowing a client to ghost you and your company; only to reach out during contract time to ask for more business, is not leadership!

In cases of the Ghost, it's important to keep in regular contact. Both you and the Ghost can decide what "regular" means ... once per month, per quarter, etc. Ask what they'd like to get out of the experience, what's their definition of a win, mesh it with your people's and/or product's ability, and recap the successes and struggles in person or remotely; following up with an email to keep in black and white for your records and theirs.

### The Looper

There will be clients that'll frequently call, email, and text you throughout your service. Some leaders enjoy working that intimately with clients; as it ensures success in the end. However, many leaders feel micro-managed, irritated, and fed-up with what I call the Looper. This client desires to be kept in the loop. Perhaps it's their first big thing and it's their baby, maybe they have trust issues, they're a perfectionist, the list of possibilities can go on!

The positive is they're invested and motivated! They care about their work and trust you to help and take it to the next level. The negative is, it's hard to get work done and complete other projects when the phone, texts, and emails keep coming in! So, what to do?

It's crucial to keep Loopers in the loop! Once you accept the Looper as a client or notice they are a Looper, share with them how you work, set a designated type and time of contact, honor it, and keep them in the loop. This will ease your mind as you will have more time to work, a designated time to discuss the project, listen to feedback, and enjoy the relationship.

The Looper will experience more peace as they have a time set to discuss their "baby", ask questions, and provide any necessary feedback. A win-win for both sides … remember, as a leader, you can become a Ghost too and that can be pretty frustrating for some of your clients!

### The Library

There are people out there that know as much as you, if not more, about your product or service … and they can become your client! The Library Client has knowledge in your field, spent time in your field, and speaks the same product language. Some have been successful, are successful; while others have the knowledge but are in transition and haven't put their knowledge into real-world practice. As a leader, you may feel excited to work with The Library, or intimidated, or irritated.

The positive is they are inspired and motivated, speak your same language, and may have experiences that will allow for a deeper connection and usefulness moving forward!

The negative can be The Library refuting your ideas, using their knowledge to elevate their ego, ignoring their lack of real-world application of their knowledge, and the list can go on. So, what to do?

As a leader, you must be clear regarding what they'd like to get out of working with you, how you can best partner, and set boundaries when necessary if you feel obligated to protect your business, your mental state, and your people from being bullied. It may sound like, "When we first began working together, you mentioned you wanted to get _____ out of working with me/us. However, when I/we do _____ it seems as if we're not on the same page. Can you help me to understand what's going on with that?". Feel free to make the statement/question more of your own.

### The Pole Vaulter

It's human nature to test, some clients will test your service boundaries by sticking their toe across your line ... while others will pole vault over your line! The Pole Vaulter is the client who continually asks for more service with no intent to compensate further, asks for more assistance in other project areas, and may reach out off-hours with the expectation you will respond and react ASAP and no matter what.

Some Pole Vaulters don't know they're pole vaulting and have deemed your professional relationship a friendship … and EXTRA is what friends do for one another. Some Pole Vaulters know exactly what they're doing and are vampires willing to suck you dry!

The positive is The Pole Vaulter wants more and sees the benefit of your talent and service! The negative is … giving is great; being taken advantage of isn't. So, what to do?

The first thing to do is to stay calm. Remember, people have only done what you've allowed! If they've been pole vaulting over your line, it's because you let them. So, don't be mad at them. I actually prefer and enjoy Pole Vaulters; as they want more … and as long as you have more to give … that's awesome!

Years ago, I had the pleasure of presenting my Leadership Training for a company and I love getting to places early. I'd go in to say hello to the leaders and wind up sitting in their office for 30 minutes chatting, talking to leadership, and answering their questions regarding issues within the organization. After I presented my training, I'd go back to their office to say goodbye and wind up staying another hour; giving away more and more information. In no way do I believe there was malice or intentional Pole-Vaulting going on; however it was happening nonetheless.

I had two choices, go in on time and leave on time; potentially decreasing and damaging the connection I built with the wonderful leaders of the company. Or, continue to arrive early as I enjoyed, engage in the conversation I enjoyed, listen to their questions (their pain-points), and answer just enough so they knew I had a solution, and follow it up with "I'd be happy to put something together for you as a training to address the issue and send over a proposal if you're interested". I went with the latter ... and more than doubled my contract with this company! The Pole-Vaulter is a GREAT client to have ... Be Mindful!

You can also choose to be more direct, "I'd love to do more. I've done _____ as extra and enjoyed it! I have an idea how we can do more and a price I think makes sense". Share your idea and provide a price range; being mindful not to lock yourself into a specific number. Your lowest number in the price range should be the number you really want. If price continues to be an issue; perhaps they can offer something in addition to money to create a win-win. In either choice, you've stated what you've done, the extra you've done, you're happy to do it, and open to discuss how to give more in a way that protects you, your relationship, and takes the pole out of their hand!

**The Ideal Client**

When I was a Mental Health Therapist,  the term for the ideal client in Y.A.V.I.S. (young, attractive, verbal, intelligent, and social). This is a client that's pleasant and easy to talk with and work with. The young or attractive part was never important to me, but I understand the point! As a leader, your ideal client will be one that's easy for you to work with ... they have just the right amount of willingness, involvement, they speak your language, trust you, the phone conversations and emails are just the right length, they listen and apply your product and service, they refer you to others, you refer them, it's perfect!

The positive is simple ... you're a perfect fit! The negative to be aware of is, you could be lulled into providing lack-luster service due to taking their idealness for granted. Here's a question ... Are you impacting them with the same energy, ideas, and service you did in the beginning or with the same vigor of trying to sign a new deal?

When you achieve your dream, my first rule of success is to take care of who and what's been taking care of you. Be sure to take care of your Ideal Clients; allowing them to stay your ideal client and YOU their ideal service!

Now that you know the 5 Types of clients, which type are you as a client? Be mindful of your positives, negatives, and what you need most! Which one resonates least with you? This is the client you may struggle with the most and need to be prepared for as a leader! Be sure to take care of your clients ... and they will take care of you!

*"Remember, people have only done what you continue to allow. If they've been pole vaulting over your line, it's because you let them. So, don't be mad at them!"*

– Andre Young

# CHAPTER 12

A Leader's Protection; 3 Ways to Protect
Your People to Success!

My youngest son plays quarterback and often finds himself in vulnerable situations in which he must open himself up to big hits to deliver the ball effectively. If you're not familiar with football, the quarterback is the person that throws the ball. They are usually the leader of the team, the most important position on the team, and are at risk of great injury due to hits they see and don't see coming. A few seasons ago, he wore rib pads for the first time for extra protection and an amazing thing happened … his confidence to stand in the pocket rose tremendously, his ability to take a hit improved, and his willingness to give a hit improved! Why? In his words … "I felt protected". What does this have to do with you, your leadership, and your organization?

It's difficult … and unlikely for people to do their best in an organization or perform their best on a team when they don't feel protected. Perhaps you've worked for a company or a boss where making a mistake led to being chewed out, disrespected, put down in front of others, demoted, or even fired. It's unlikely you'd want to take a risk again; nor would anyone else within the organization. It's hard to grow a business or successful team this way; and you may promote managers … but not leaders!

Throughout this book, you've read my thoughts on protection and how it fits into your leadership. Here are 3 ways to protect your people to success:

**Create Opportunities for Success**

This sounds simple, but several things go into this step to enhance your Leadership & Work/Life Harmony and that of your people:

1. Know your Vision & Vision Factors for success. It's hard to know what success is and when you've achieved it personally, professionally, and within your organization when you haven't defined it.

2. Know what skills, attitude, and success you want and need from your people. Be sure they are aware too!

3. Know the superpowers of your people; what do they bring to the table? Are they aware? Does their perceived superpower match their true ability or potential? When it matches, great! When it doesn't, it's time to have a tough and honest conversation that protects you, them, and the team. This leads us to number 4…

4. Are your people in the right seat within your team or organization to allow success?

5. Consistently educate and provide training for you people to enhance their skills, their leadership, and their work/life harmony; allowing them the opportunity to progress with you or after you.

We live in a new era; most employees that start with you will not finish with you. It's not that they're disloyal ... it's simply the way of today! While they're with you ... give them a reason to stay longer and make them great... so when they leave the world must take notice of the type of people coming from your organization. Believe me, it will pay off as great people will acknowledge your organization and want to be a part of it!

**Embrace Failure**

This is the opposite of the example I shared earlier of the person being chewed out after making a mistake. As a leader, create a culture where thinking outside the box is encouraged, manageable risk is encouraged, and lessons from failure are nourished!

Of course, we all want 100% wins, but that's not realistic! So how do you embrace failure?

Share with your people the importance of thinking big or bigger ... assuming this is something you want to do. Encourage a sharing of ideas with coworkers, leaders, and everyone. Explain there will be times when you will go with their idea, there may be times you collaborate, and times you cannot go with their idea due to bigger picture issues.

It's also necessary to give your people enough rope to succeed or fail. Although you're encouraging free and big thinking ... it doesn't mean your employees are running around like chickens with their heads cut off, doing any and every idea, and doing whatever they want. Establish a process of sharing ideas and starting ideas ... this process cannot pass through too many desks; otherwise, a lot of nothing happens! Also, if the damage of a new idea and risk is minimal (you must decide what minimal is) provide your people permission to JUST DO IT and report back afterward. Here are a few questions to ask:

1. What was good about the idea or what you did? What did you like about it?
2. What did you learn from it?
3. What advice would you give someone doing it in the future

This is a perfect opportunity to protect your people, your leadership, and enhance their leadership; as you allow an employee to share the experience and their answers to the questions above in your next meeting. This is how success, growth, and evolution happen and is encouraged!

**Success Map**

Remember, leaders protect their people from themselves ... as not everyone is overly ambitious and "Inspired & Motivated". Many managers, employees, and team members will drone about when left to their own accord ... therefore, create a Success Map for your people!

A Success Map is a plan to show those on your team or in your organization how to achieve their professional definition of success! This suggests you are curious enough to ask and know their answer. Perhaps they want to be you one day and sit in your seat. Maybe they want to open a bakery, but need this current job until their dream is a real possibility. Either way ... great! Most employees have no idea all of the wonderful things their company can offer. As a professional speaker, I get to meet incredible people all over the world. Some I can impact right away within my area of expertise. Others desire input outside of my wheelhouse, and I get to refer. Therefore, I'm honored to always be of value ... and so can you and your organization!

*"As a leader, create a culture where thinking outside the box is encouraged, manageable risk is encouraged, and lessons from failure are nourished"*

– Andre Young

# CHAPTER 13

# A Leader's List; Know & Respect the Lists of Your People!

You know that tornado of "Things-To-Do" swirling around your head? If you're in a professional position of leadership … you've got a list and that list tends to make you "Busy". Please remember, "Busy" does not mean "Better" and "Busy" doesn't mean "Productive". Also, your people have a list of their own … ignoring this fact as a leader can cause burn-out, bore-out, and damage your Leadership & Work/Life Harmony and theirs! So, what to do?

### You're People's List

One of the biggest mistakes made by the even noblest of leaders is not knowing the lists' of their people. Leaders tend to ask employees to do things and believe the only thing on that person's list is their job and the tasks you asked them to do. Completely oblivious you asked them to do three things, but so did Mike, Jen, and Bob from down the hall! Therefore, their list isn't three things long … it's twelve things longs + the things they were previously working on to get their actual job done. Then … the death blow comes when you, as the leader, ask the employee, "Why isn't the task done?" … and they either melt inside themselves feeling inadequate and overwhelmed, or they explode in frustration and are now deemed a problem employee! In my experience, the best way I've found to be aware of my people's list was the 1-on-1 Meetings explained in Chapter 9. It allows you to be your version of "Busy", them to be their version of "Busy", with a date scheduled on the calendar to review and prioritize the "Busy"; most people can hold on when they know help is coming … be Mindful!

**What If You're the Employee**

As an employee or team member, you have a list … a list of your duties, extras asked of you by your boss, favors requested by coworkers, etc. Please remember you have options and leadership is a two-way street!

You have the option to suffer in silence; taking on more and more responsibilities until you burn-out. You have the option of not assuming enough responsibility until you bore-out. Most employees in either situation begin to gripe to other coworkers, significant others, friends, and eventually anyone who will listen about their work issues. This venting makes sense in the moment; however, what you think about all day impacts how you feel, how you behave, your actions, and finally your consequences. It's hard to think and talk negatively about your job all day and love it! So, what to do?

**Burnt-Out Options:**

You're stressed and have taken on too much! Request time to speak with your boss 1-on-1; perhaps schedule a time to respect their daily list. Share your list of tasks and your idea of what the top 1-3 priorities are; as well as your plan to address them. Ask your boss what they like about your idea and what they'd fine-tune. This not only shares your list; it also shows your leadership and initiative to problem solve and ask for guidance. Remember, your boss may be unaware of how long your list really is ... and it may also show just how valuable you really are!

Option two, ask for help to best prioritize your list. Share your list and ask for clarification on the "Bigger-Picture" to better organize your list. Too often, employees prioritize tasks based on who gave them the task. The CEO may give a task that's not relevant for six weeks; while a coworker requested a favor that helps to make next week's deadline. The CEO has the title, but not making the deadline costs the company their best client. Requesting the "Bigger-Picture" not only helps you prioritize; it forces your leaders to lead!

The last option, you can continue complaining to whoever will listen and venting at work, becoming a Negative Nick or Nancy; droning about your job for decades or soon to be out of a job with no positive Letter of Recommendation to help you move forward. Many have done it and I don't think many would recommend it in retrospect!

**Bored-Out Option:**

You're droning about at your job, believing you can do more, and ready to be more! Request time with your boss 1-on-1; perhaps schedule a time to respect their daily list. Share your passion to be of increased value to the company/team. It may sound like, "Thank

You for making time to meet with me. I wanted to say I enjoy working here and would like to be of more value. I have an idea that may help and would like to know what you like about it … or your ideas of how I can do more." Feel free to make this statement your own, but be sure to thank them for their time, be sure to have completed the tasks you're actually getting paid to do, and be open to brainstorming. Be mindful … what you may want to do may not be what the organization/team needs most right now.

When you have a specific idea of what you'd like to do for the organization/team, share it out of a willingness to add value; not putting down other people, bosses, or departments.

If you don't have an exact idea, express an interest to learn more about various aspects of the organization and ask for more ways to be involved. The best-case scenario is … you get what you asked for! You and your boss may collaborate on an idea. Or, your idea may be rejected. This doesn't mean they are rejecting you as a person … rather, rejecting your idea for an array of possible reasons! Perhaps your idea doesn't fit into the Vision & Vision Factors, the organization is strict in its policies, they struggle to think outside the box, or your boss is an abusive jerk. Either way, you will eventually know what type of organization you work for and will have a choice to stay or read the writing on the wall and begin looking elsewhere. If you choose to stay, it makes no sense to be angry about what you know to be true. If you decide to leave, it makes no sense to be angry about something you get to leave!

Here's a final tip for all employees … you add value by relieving pain! Know where the organization/team is falling short, know your superpower, and how that superpower can best add value to stop the pain. Propose your solution and a win-win … what's the win for them, a win for you, and how soon can it begin? "A Win" for the organization may be one less problem to address, increased productivity, saving money, or increasing revenue. Perhaps a "Win" for you is experience to put on your resume, knowing more about the organization, learning a desirable skill, a raise, a promotion, a new title, etc. A friend once told me, "When you raise your value higher than your customer's stack of money, you'll always be ok!". I've never forgotten that and it's true as an employee, leader, and entrepreneur!

*"One of the biggest mistakes made by the even noblest of leaders is not knowing the lists of their people."*
– Andre Young

# CHAPTER 14

# A Leader's Speed Bump; How to Best Lead Your "Speedy Employee"!

As a leader, either you've come across or will come across what I call a "Speedy Employee". This is the person on your team that's a go-getter, doesn't need micro-managing, is intuitive, listens, applies, takes initiative, and hits the ground running; all you have to do is point them in the right direction! In my employee years, I was the "Speedy Type". I wanted to GO; therefore, I asked questions and wrote whatever answer my boss or trainer gave in a notebook I carried around … so I only had to ask once, I could learn on the fly, and develop my craft. Sounds like a great employee to have on your team, right? Remember, they're Pros & Concerns to everything! The Pro is your "Speedy Employee" can be an asset as they help to impact and enhance the vision and expectations you have for your team; acting as a model for how to be and a beacon of professionalism servicing your clientele. However, The Concern is, they will only do as good as their leader allows, delegates, and deals with the mistakes "The Speedy Employee" will inherently make!

Too often, leaders may become frustrated by "The Speedy Employee" because they want to move too fast, learn too much, take initiative, mistakenly operate outside of the chain of command, or simply make a mistake they were bold enough to attempt and invest themselves in. I've heard and seen leaders rudely reprimand "The Speedy Employee" in email or face-to-face … or visibly become upset or intimated by "The Speedy's" drive and enthusiasm. A boss once yelled at me for being too happy … Yes, this really happened! Or, a supervisor has checked-out or burntout, and leading this type of employee is no longer what they desire to do; as your "Speedy Employee" quietly demands more from your leadership.

As long as your "Speedy Employee" is coming from a place of wanting to do great at their job, has the best interest of the team at heart, and is motivated to DO and BE more…. your job as a leader is to evolve their process; not stifle their progress. So, how do you do that?

**Their Dream?**

It's so important to connect with your "Speedy Employee" at this level! Know what their dream is and what they want to get out of working with you, for you, and at the organization. When their dream has anything or nothing to do with the organization … Great! The truth is, an employee like this will not be with you or under you forever; they inevitably will move up or move on. When they move up … it helps the company and your reputation that you had something to do with it. Again, when they move on … and you knew their dream and either helped them with it or at least encouraged it; this allows them to speak great about you in their new professional and personal world ... and your company will be seen as a great place to work!

Be mindful ... one day, you may end up working as a leadership peer or under "The Speedy Employee"; crazier things have happened! In my first job out of college, I was young and speedy and my supervisor was a great guy. I learned a few nuggets from him I still use to this day. I later accepted a new job at a new company, loved it, and rose to a leadership position. Who knew ... five years later, a man was hired to be a part of my team and who walked in but my old supervisor! Wow, I suddenly became his supervisor!

### How They Learn?

Your "Speedy Employee" knows how they learn best ... do you and can you make room for it? In my Leadership Training Program, I talk about A Leader's Nicely ... the four big ways people learn best and which type you are and your people are. Know yours, know theirs, and allow a marriage of the two.

Remember the notebook I said I carried around to ask questions only once? I can't tell you how many bosses told me to put my notebook away during my first few weeks on a job. They told me to put it away and that I wouldn't need it! Why? Perhaps it's the first time they've seen someone do it, subconsciously expect you to learn as they learn, or maybe the process slowed down their teaching. The point is, how do you like to teach, how do they learn best, marry the two, and allow for great learning to positively impact your team and company!

### Clear Expectations!

Your "Speedy Employee" is intuitive, listens to what is needed, responds quickly to requests, and is off to the races! They are most likely going to do the task within the guidelines initially presented to them and honor the titles within the organization. Sometimes, their speedy follow-through can inadvertently mess things up. Or, when YOUR boss asks them to do something ... they're most likely to speed to get it done. However, to you ... it may look as if they've overstepped boundaries and the chain of command. Let's face it, sometimes your boss has no idea of what's really going on, the nitty-gritty details, and the relationships you have with those involved in the project ... and here they come with a bright idea, request, or a change of plans ... giving it to you're "Speedy Employee" and now it's more work for you to clean up. Sound familiar?

The problem is, due to your emotion of the minute, you may take it out on your "Speedy Employee"; lashing out at them rather than having the necessary conversation with your boss. As a leader, it's your job to set clear expectations with your boss AND with your "Speedy Employee".

1. Set a time to discuss with your boss how the project is working and it will be completed better and faster when requests can be made through you and delegated through you as you have the inside track, relationships, and plan to put everyone in the right seats to get the job done. As a leader, when a backdoor approach is needed ... It may be best to present it as an idea. "I have an idea I think would help with the communication problem we just had with the project or __(person)__. It's been working best when you contact me with the issue or request and I deliver it to ___(person)___. Due to the nature of the project, I have a lot of inside information and can help us save some time and potentially some money. Plus, it helps me in my posi-

tion as the team leader to enhance my skills and that of my team". Feel free to make this more of your own.

2.  Have a positive conversation to appreciate your "Speedy Employee's" diligence in getting tasks done and share the expectations of how to best handle interference by others or higher-ups in the company. So, how to do it?

**The Positive Sandwich!**

Think about the anxiety your "Speedy Employee" may feel for not following through on a task YOUR boss asked them to do. That's why it's NECESSARY you exhibit great leadership by addressing this with your boss first; to protect your "Speedy Employee" then address it with him/her to fine-tune the process; ensuring leadership, teamwork, and elite customer satisfaction!

In the mishap I shared above ... remember, your "Speedy Employee" was simply doing what they were asked to do, getting the job done as usual, and being a great employee. However, that will not erase your frustration and the amount of clean-up you now have to do. Therefore, having a conversation when you're in the middle of your emotion is not typically a good idea. The last thing you want to do is turn an employee who cares into an employee who doesn't. Schedule a time with "The Speedy" to discuss. Be mindful of having this conversation via email; as leaders protect themselves and you may not prefer to have statements about the intrusion of other leaders in black and white, Lol!

The Positive Sandwich may sound like, "I'm glad we're getting to talk. You're a great worker and the team benefits from how quickly you're getting things done. As you can see, there can be a lot of hands in the pot and sometimes when someone who is not closely involved with a project asks you to do something, it can cause unforeseen issues. I don't want you to stop being how you are. As we move forward, I'd like you to reach out to me first when _____ requests you to _____ and we can go from there with either you doing the task or I can step in. I've addressed this with _____ and we appreciate all the work you're doing!".  This conversation completes the circle, as you've met with your boss, protected your leadership, the organization, and customer-base ... and met with your "Speedy Employee. Job well done!

*"As a leader, sometimes you may have to evolve someone's process, but never stifle their progress ... Be Mindful!"*
– Andre Young

# CHAPTER 15

# A Leader's Rock & A Hard Place; How to Lead When Stuck Between Upper Management and a High Performer!

Middle Management can be hard! It's one of the first promotions into a position of leadership. Higher-ups have seen your professional worth and believe you have what it takes to lead. It's an exciting time; full of pride, anxiety, and the ever-lasting pressure of meeting the desires and sometimes unrealistic expectations of those above you ... along with the task to lead those under you! In a perfect world, you and upper management are on the same page, patient, and willing to brainstorm to build together, while the front-line employees love their jobs, accept all duties, and changes without a problem ... Yeah right!

Perhaps you and upper management aren't on the same page; you're frustrated and need to get the job done. Higher-Ups have set the expectation, but you have front-line superstars that do their own thing and are more protected professionally than you are. This happens in sports quite a bit … The owner likes a certain player, pays him/her a lot of money, the player performs, the coach's job is to make it work … even though the player breaks all the rules, is a locker room nightmare, and is uncoachable … sound familiar at your job? So, what to do?

### "The Meeting"

As the person in the middle, the first step is to meet with the top! It's essential to be on the same page … as much as possible. Remember, your job and professional advancement may depend on it. Whether you stay at the job or venture elsewhere; news of your reputation will travel … Be sure it's saying what you want it to say!

In your meeting with Upper Management, it's your goal to walk out of the room or close your laptop with a more clear understanding of a few powerful things:

1. What's the exact mission of my job? – Get clear on what you're expected to do and accomplish.

2. How much control do you have within your position? A leadership position with zero decision-making abilities may quickly become a position of frustration. How far does your rope extent to make decisions? What issues or decisions need to be discussed with upper management first before you can act on an employee's issues?

3. What do we agree on regarding upper management's Leader's 3 and yours … sharing best ways to lead through employee infractions? It may be a great idea to ask Upper Management what they like about your Leader's 3 and anything they'd fine-tune.

Whether you agreed with the conversation's outcome or not ... the answers to these questions will provide you more clarity, direction, and confidence moving forward. However, it will not always play out this simple and like with everything, there are outliers. That All-Star employee that's a high-performer and doesn't have to follow the rules, that employee that was hired as a family favor and will never get fired, or the employee that has all the potential in the world but never reaches it and hurts the team with mistake after mistake after mistake. I could go on, but you get it!

I've had the pain and privilege of working with and leading all three types and have been professionally impacted by them all; as I'm sure you have! The All-Star is undeniable ... you see their talent and potential to be the best at what they do. As a leader, praise their ability and let them know the intention of your role is to help fine-tune their skills for success and to help overcome the pitfalls you know are coming that they struggle to forsee. When I was a Mental Health Therapist working in an Alternative School, I worked with a gentleman that was an all-star connector and was eager to fix every issue for every student and every staff. My job became helping him to hone his skills, teach him how to teach other staff to do what he did; allowing others to improve ... all in efforts to enhance the entire team and save him from certain burn-out and frustration when the luster of the job begins to fade.

I've worked under the "Family-Hire"; a good person, but a terrible fit for the position ... and he was not going to get fired! I'm sad to say, I did not behave my best. I grew frustrated quickly, vented to anyone who'd listen, disconnected from my team and my passion, became the worst version of myself professionally, and was presented with an option to transfer sites. Looking back, it was the turning point of my professional life; leading me to the very beginning of what I am today as a professional speaker, author, and leadership trainer ... So, it all worked out! However, I still wish I had handled it better.

Lastly, I employed "The Potential" and let way too many things slide; negatively impacting my leadership and reputation. He was a good person, however not every good person is a good fit ... Lesson learned! So, how do you connect, build, and move forward under this type of stress?

### The Marriage

It's now time to connect and bond with the person causing you so many headaches and sleepless nights ... "The High Performer"! I know it sounds dramatic, but isn't it? I recommend a marriage; all with the vision to create your desired professional lifestyle predicated on communication, big-vision habits, positivity, and follow-through. To achieve this, you have two choices:

1.  *"The Jimmy Johnson Approach"* – Jimmy Johnson is most famous for being the Head Coach of the Dallas Cowboys in the 1990's, winning three Superbowls, and creating one of the most prolific dynasties of all time. His approach to leadership with star players was tough ... but not necessarily fair or equal. It's reported he told his team ... the stars will be treated differently and had a longer rope than everyone else. It was also reported, he shared with his superstars when he planned to yell at them in front of the team and explained the purpose was to impact on everyone; making back-up players aware they'd better not even think of making a mistake! Agree or disagree ... he was upfront and consistent. Granted, this approach has some concerns as star professionals can use extra rope to hang themselves.

2.  *The Marriage* – involves sitting with your high-performer to share:

- The impact their abilities and high potential can have for them as individuals, for the team, and for their future
- Increase your understanding of what they want to get out of working for you and with you? Why are they there? Help to develop their Vision & Vision Factors (The 3-5 things that when done consistently will make the vision come true)
- Share your Vision & Vision Factors as a leader
- Marry your goals
- Agree to become a team; exhibiting a combined vision, plan, expectations, and rules that can be revisited regularly to maintain the relationship and the goal

**Follow Through**

I know the above sounds "cheesy," and it doesn't always work as neatly as I described. However, what does? The truth is … this meeting is simply the beginning … and when done with sincerity, is powerful! In the real world, what happens next usually tanks results … you get busy as a leader and neglect to follow up, maintain 1-on-1 connection, and the relationship never gets to flourish. Or, you get busy and during times of high stress … revert to what you know … and behave accordingly. Don't be so "Busy" being "Busy" that you forget to build and be better!

After you've had "The Meeting", "The Marriage", now it's time to Follow Through with your regular 1-on-1 Meetings. When things are still not going the way you like … sad to say, but the job may not be for you and you have a choice to make.

You can gripe, pout, or vent your frustrations to anyone who'll listen … and believe me; you will always find someone to listen and agree with you. However, it will not change the reality of your situation ... and will make it worse over time as your negative thoughts and words will eventually drip into your actions ... making you a part of the problem!

Therefore, the option to enhance your Leadership & Work/ Life Harmony is to understand and marry YOUR WHY. When you choose to stay in a position that's stressing you out ... Why are you still at that job? Whatever your reason ... money, advancement opportunities, gained experience, etc ... Marry your "Why"! Know what you're getting out of showing up every day! Next, enhance your Superpower; whatever you're good at ... get great at! If things get better at work ... you'll be noticed as part of the solution. If things get worse and you leave ... you'll leave as an asset; not a liability. Next, enjoy your relationships and network better ... Who do you enjoy at work? Who's positive, productive, and inspiring ... spend your time with them and enjoy your day or work experience! Lastly, when all has failed; the writing is on the wall and it may be time to walk away with your head held high and eagerly ready for the next chapter of your professional and personal life!

> *"As a leader, it's important to know ... Not every good person*
> *is a good fit, and that's OK"*
> – Andre Young

# CHAPTER 16

# A Leader's Gossip; 4 Ways to Lead Through the Inevitable!

Gossip … What a powerfully destructive word; yet it seems to be a mainstay in the way many employees converse in the workplace, at home, and in their relationships. You've experienced it during your work breaks … engaging in, listening to, or overhearing gossip about your boss, coworkers, the projects, and all of the decisions you think are dumb. Only to return home or close your laptop and share it all over again with your significant other, family, and friends. Or, you leave your friends … and it's seemingly more natural to gossip about people rather than smile and recap the positives of the night.

That's the problem with gossip … it tends to only deal with the negatives or perceived negatives; it prevents us from truly enjoying and valuing our job, work, or relationships over weeks, months, years, and decades of talking poorly about them … it's hard to love them and give your all. Lastly, gossiping negatively impacts your reputation as a leader and may significantly erode your chances to advance at work. What's negatively said and heard rarely gets forgotten and can unwittingly keep you stuck professionally. So, what to do? Here are 4 Ways to attack gossip and block the gossiping of others!

**Be Mindful!**

As a leader, you will have your good days and tough days. I don't like saying "Bad Days'" as this world consists of roughly 7 billion people and more than half of them would trade places with you right now; gladly taking what you call a "Bad Day"! Be Mindful to openly discuss and positively gossip about the good you see in the organization, your team, your people, your boss, and coworkers. Let people overhear you saying something great about others and let that "Good Gossip" travel as fast as the bad gossip! It's amazing how it hits your employees, your boss, your husband, or wife that you were talking good about them. As a professional speaker, it's one of the compliments I get and am most proud of ... "I love the way you talk about your wife!". The audience likes hearing my "Good Gossip" and honestly ... it's hard to speak positively and lovingly about someone or something all day long then go home and not like them. Your words are powerful ... Be Mindful!

The second big point is ... on those "Tough Days", Be Mindful of who, when, and where you choose to vent! This cannot be understated ... be sure your venting is people-limited, time-limited, purposeful ... and done in the right setting.

Leaders are human too and venting will happen from time to time and now you know how to do it. Gossiping is the opposite and doesn't have to happen; when you do decide to engage; make it "Good Gossip" and let that spread ... believe me, you won't be on the wrong end of receiving a "Tough Conversation" from your

Higher-Ups when that's the case! A leader who engages in the bad gossip breaks the trust of their team, loses their team, encourages the behavior, and will tend to get the bare minimum from their people; manufacturing other gossipers and cliques.

## Listen Positive!

You may not be the gossiper, but what will you do when gossip comes your way … and it will? Every job has its Negative Nicks and Nancys and they want to talk to YOU! They'll share their story of woe about things, people, and decisions they don't like at work or in their personal lives … and will speak for as long as you're willing to listen. Saying nothing doesn't make you innocent … actively listening day after day makes you just as much a part of the problem … just like the Get-Away Driver that didn't shoot anyone or steal anything! So, what to do?

## The Bold Approach

A Gossiper starts their teardown of the company, team, or person and you say … "I hear you; I'm glad I'm not in _____(person's)_____ position. They have tough decisions to make and probably didn't even fully like or agree with this one and still have to deliver it to us with a smile." … and walk away!!! I've used this in my employee days with coworkers and many of them simply looked at me, nodded their heads, and said "hmmm". That's what I call an "Eye-Brow Raising Moment"!

## The Subtle Approach

I've done this one as well. A Gossiper starts their teardown of the company, team, or person and in mid-sentence, I'd say, "I'm sorry, excuse me, I have to get something from the printer (or whatever/wherever) I'll be back".… and never come back, Lol!

The point is to get away from the drama, negativity, and gossip to protect your sanity, your professionalism, and your leadership as your name will not pop up in the gossip and garbage!

**The Gossip Choice**

We all have three choices when it comes to the urge to gossip. You and I are human and will face it daily, professionally, personally, and your Leadership & Work/Life Harmony depends on the choices you consistently make.

Vent & Initiate – Again, be sure your venting is people-limited, time-limited, purposeful, and with a plan to initiate a new and positive way to address the issue. One of my BIG Rules is to please accompany your problem with a suggested solution!

Vent & Accept – Vent appropriately and read the writing on the wall. In the example I shared earlier in the book about becoming a burnt-out employee due to organizational transition; I saw nothing was going to change and inevitably become worse. Although I was wrong about how I said my gossip and who I said it to … I was right about the problems and instead of corporate addressing the issuses, people, and processes; they were full speed ahead on what I disagreed with. Therefore, I had a choice and you have a choice to vent like a leader and either accept what is, adjust and stay … or accept what is, prepare, and move on to a job or profession more suitable with your vision. There's no sense arguing and being a cog in the system when you know you're leaving and will most likely need a letter of recommendation!

Vent & Evolve – This isn't for everyone, but some leaders and employees desire to have their own, start their own, and be their own boss one day. What a great position you're in to enhance your craft and superpower, learn what to do, what not to do, vent appropriately, and evolve as you prepare to begin your own business.

This option provides so much clarity as you get to fully utilize your good and bad experiences from the job you currently dislike … and it also offers more appreciation and understanding for all the bosses, employees, projects, and changes you gossiped about! The gift of being on both sides tends to assist your professional and personal perspective and evolution!

**A Reset**

My expectation in my business is simple … Positivity, Passion, & Productivity. I only hire or outsource individuals that are positive in mindset and language, a joy to work with, energetic, great at their job, intuitive, proactive, and produce toward the vision. Gossip and negative talk have NO place in what I just described. Your team and organization may be in need of a Reset of what's expected, respected, and accepted; however, it only sticks when you model it and consequence it. Enjoy the journey and your new view on A Leader's Gossip!

*"Let people overhear you saying something great about others and let that "Good Gossip" travel as fast as the bad!"*
– Andre Young

# CHAPTER 17

# A Leader's Let Go; Firing Your Two Biggest Employee Pain-Points!

Firing ... this is a sensitive topic and let's face it, it's hard to get fired in America but shouldn't be impossible or done too late. You may have read or heard me say in my Leadership Videos, "Leadership is not for the weak"; and you can be sure your leadership will be tested! When you're in a leadership position, there will come a time you will be challenged and faced with the dilemma to have the direct and tough conversation with an employee ... or not. As difficult, irritating, or anxiety-producing it may be... believe me, it will become even more difficult and irritating when you don't!

Remember, everyone that starts with you, your team, and your vision ... may not end with you! Perhaps their interests have changed for professional or personal reasons, your goals and vision are no longer aligned, their interactions with others are poor, their skill set is no longer conducive to achieving the vision and mis-

sion, and the many other reasons why this individual may no longer be a good fit. Whatever the reason, there are two main types
of employees that must be held accountable and sometimes let go.

I'd like to preface this by stating the overwhelming importance that YOU as the leader must hold yourself accountable first
… then EVERYONE else. Now, who are the two main types of
employees to beware; "The Potential" and The High Performer!

### "The Potential"

This is the individual you knew did not have all of the knowledge, the skills needed, or experience for the job but was impres-
sively eager to tackle it! You gave them a shot, yet their best shot
has not been enough; and even worse … is damaging to your business, the team, your reputation, and the organization. Their lack of
improvement could be on you as a leader … a lack of coaching provided or training offered, not knowing or respecting how they learn
best, being too busy to walk them through projects, or your failure
to provide a safe space for them to ask questions. Be sure to explore
this avenue first, as YOU are the leader and most responsible.

Years ago, my business model was different. I wanted to be of
impact and enhance the lives of people everywhere. After years
of doing it alone, I hired a staff that became a fantastic team. I
focused on adults in the community while my staff of twelve (4
adults and 8 college interns) serviced two college campuses. I personally trained and supervised everyone and it was great and hard
all at the same time! Long story short, there was an intern that
was motivated, high-energy, passionate, and had all the potential
in the world. However, I never knew which version of him I was
going to get! While doing the job of impacting young lives, he was
great. However, as soon as the gavel banged (so to speak) and the
session ended, he switched and I could hear him spouting foul

language and making rude comments. We had conversations on remaining consistent and him needing to choose which version of himself he wanted to be, because I could only continue to employ one of them. I allowed this to go on for a while due to his charm and potential.

One evening, while I was present to observe a Life-Enrichment Session on the campus, I noticed he was conducting it while under the influence. Although I couldn't prove it ... I could feel my other employees and the attendees being very aware and uncomfortable. We concluded the session, I met with him the following day, and we had an honest conversation about the incident. Although he denied being under the influence ... MY BIGGEST MISTAKE WAS NOT LETTING HIM GO! As a leader, your BIG HEART or being uncomfortable can get the best of you ... but that's not the best for your employee or the team.

I remember seeing my team after the meeting and feeling so small. Do you know the standard and expectation it would have set if I had done the process I'm about to share with you now? Needless to say, I've never made that mistake again as I put desired culture first and understand one big thing ... employees who have done wrong tend to know they've done wrong and are expecting to have a tough conversation with a leader and receive consequences or at least a warning. When this doesn't occur ... you've given the green light for it to continue!

### The High-Performer

Have you ever worked on a team that had a High-Performer? Their numbers, their output, or however your organization measures success, are out of this world! High-Performers are great and every organization and team wants them and needs them. However, is your high-performer helpful or harmful?

Whether it's sports or a traditional work environment, Helpful High-Performers succeed and also raise the level of performance of those around them. The Helpful Type doesn't mind connecting, coaching, and celebrating the success of others. The individual wins, the team wins, and the organization wins!

The Harming High-Performer is quite different. Outside of impressive numbers and output, they operate like a shark! Although they are good at what they do and outside of the workplace may be an enjoyable person ... they bully, lie, and/or steal clients and customers to single-handedly profit to climb the ladder of success. They may be in a leadership position within your company and are verbally abusive and micro-managing to your staff. This may be your most productive salesperson; their numbers are good, but when you look at WHY, it's mixed with their ability and effort ... but also a pattern of abusive and subversive tactics.

The saddest part is ... typically, the organization knows it's going on ... but because the numbers are so good the organization fears not being able to hire a qualified replacement ... Therefore, nothing changes!

The truth is, there are roughly 7.5 billion people on the planet. Although it will be annoying to find someone else, it will disrupt the project, you'd have to train someone new ... in the long run, it's possible, worth it, and needs to happen! Remember, your people are watching and will know what's really important to you and the organization based on your action or inaction. So, what's the process of Letting Go of "The Potential" and "The High-Performer"?

1.  Provide Feedback – Do this regularly and honestly. I've shared the process and significance of having A Leader's 1-on-1 Meetings and implore you to do so with your "Potential" and "High-Performer"!

2. Seek Understanding – Why are they engaging in what you consider to be problematic behaviors? They may not see it as problematic; they may have done this same behavior in every job they've ever had. Perhaps they've never been told not to; mimicking the sub-culture of the organization that you don't see. Whether they shine a light on something or hang themselves with their own words … seek to understand as you will learn more about them, the sub-culture of your team, and your leadership!

3. Set Expectations – This is monumentally important. Have you set an expectation that an abuse of power, abusive language, stealing clients/customers, lying, micro-managing, etc. is against the expectations of your leadership, the team, and the desired culture? Remember, your people don't know what you don't say!

4. Rules – What are they? There doesn't need to be many, but there needs to at least be a few. Being clear and consistent with your rules will make your leadership easier; creating win-wins for your organization. A win "The Potential" or "High-Performer" can take their skills to the next level to benefit their success and the company's … or, a win that will take "The Potential" or "High-Performer" to a new company; leaving a gap for you to fill with someone more aligned with your vision!

5. Follow-Through – When feedback is ignored, expectations and rules are not respected, it's time to follow through and let these individuals go. This will be tough as you either like this person, their ability is impressive, you've invested so much time and money into them, or they bring in so much revenue. Remember, sports teams do this all the time … with the mindset of creating a productive and cohesive

team positioned to win championships. Teams with great individual players may win games, but not always championships. You want great people with great ability that are a best fit for your vision and system!

6. The actual Follow Through Conversation may sound something like this, "Hi _____, thank you for coming in for the meeting today. It's been good having you here at _____. However, given the ongoing conversations we've had over the past few _____(weeks/ months/years)_____ regarding ____(examples)_____. We/I've decided to let you go. I believe this can be a win for you as your positives are _____(list one or two)_____. However, we're looking for someone more aligned with our vision, expectations, and rules. Thank you for your time with us and I truly wish you well".

7. Feel free to use this statement or make it your own. Be sure to thank them for their service, effort, and time with you. Mention the conversations had in the past about said behaviors … as they can't be denied. Be clear you're letting them go, share they may be a better fit elsewhere, and what you are looking for in an employee and why. Remember, this conversation will not be a shock to them when you've consistently shared the vision, expectations, and rules, had your 1-on-1's, and had the casual and tough conversations along the way.

Once you've followed through and let go … it's imperative to inform your team and share the WHY! This is not a time to bash and degrade; rather a time to reexplain your Leader's 3 … and a plan to unify until a suitable replacement arrives. This is a time of possibility and opportunity as employees may have to share work, get promoted, learn something new, and shift ... but all done in a new and positive environment. Be mindful that some may like the change, some may not ... however, the new expectation and direction has been set!

*"Your people are watching and will know what's really important to you and the organization based on your action or inaction ... Be Mindful!"*
– Andre Young

A Leader's Passion ... Plus

*Leadership takes passion;*
*plus a few more things!*

CHAPTER 18

# A Leader's New Normal; How to
# Accept Evolution!

Evolution rarely feels good or something you easily accept when it begins; rather, it feels like change ... and change can be annoying! Professionally and personally, change can be anticipated and accepted or can be thrusted upon you and viewed as unfair and frustrating; as you focus on what was lost instead of taking advantage of the gains. Organizations worldwide experienced this with a global pandemic (COVID-19); change was forced, many suffered, and leaders and organizations had to evolve or die! Lives were changed as people were home together unabated for months at a time and relationships had to evolve or die! I can go on but you get the point! Whether it's a global pandemic or something on a smaller scale ... there will always be something lurking around the corner to gut-punch your organization, your team, and your life. Leaders are able to accept the new normal quicker than others and allow evolution to work in their favor. So, how do you do it?

During the COVID-19 Pandemic, I was finishing up a Leadership Training with an organization and a leader asked, "How do we get back to normal?". My response shot out of my mouth while my thoughts were going a mile a minute ... "Are you sure that's what you want?". He was well-intentioned with his question; as he cared for the organization, his people, and the mission, however he did want most people do ... romanticize the past!

**The Past**

The organization in this scenario and your organization have a past ... and that past had some great qualities or your company wouldn't exist now. That past has some mediocre qualities that could've been improved if everyone wasn't so busy ... and some bad qualities that would have benefited from being addressed, changed, or scrapped if it wasn't for the "We've always done it this way Approach"! The same happens when we explore our lives and relationships. We tend to resist change and the possibility for evolution because we get stuck romanticizing the past or become comfortable in our "Busy"!

When you choose to view the past as a leader, ask yourself, your team, your employees, or those in your personal life these questions and simply listen:

1. What aspects did you like about _____ from before the change hit and snowballed?
2. Is there anything we could have been doing differently before the change that would have made us better, more productive, or more prepared for the change?

Asking and answering these questions will get you out of sulking mode and into Evolving Mode! Remember, trying to recreate what was will only take you away from what is and can be! The past and the way of doing things is gone ... although sad and frustrating; it can be the start of a new and better chapter. What did you like from the past; is it possible and does it make sense to bring some things from the past back? If yes, great! If not, admire it and let evolution take its course! What could have been done to make you or your organization more ready for the transition ... know the answer and proactively include strategies to improve and prepare for the next change coming. As a leader, you don't know exactly what the next change will be, but the writing is usually on the wall ... sometimes in BIG BOLD PRINT and sometimes in the small fine print. Great leaders anticipate, prepare, and go!

**The Present**

Change has happened, the past is gone, and here you are! The present is where you live, where your organization is, and our action or inaction during this time will dictate the future ... so let's go! When I went through my biggest life transitions; a divorce, a job change after fifteen years, preparing to start my own business, and most recently ... transitioning my services to the virtual world ... the best and most meaningful three things I chose to do was:

1. Keep Your Eyes Wide Open! I use this saying often when going through change (wanted or unwanted) and share it with individuals I coach ... keep your eyes wide open and take a good look and the new! It can never hurt more than the first time you see it. Through this process, gain an understanding of what you did great, what you did good

but could have improved, and what you did bad and need to stop ... making a plan for how to best move forward!

2. Know your skillset! Know what you do best, what you have to offer, and have a vision for your success professionally and personally!

3. Things have changed; therefore peoples' needs or how they desire to receive what you serve may have changed. Know it, be willing, and able to deliver! Knowing the needs of who you're serving, whether it's your organization, your team, your customer, or significant other ... it never gets old and will pay you back ten-fold!

Let's look at this professionally and personally ... before COVID-19, organizations wanted leadership training for their people. However, when COVID hit it took a toll on the company budget, fewer people were doing more work due to constant lay-offs and furloughs, then sadly George Floyd was murdered and Race & Diversity became paramount, and people were too busy for any training that wasn't Race & Diversity, tech-related, or Zoom related. That's a lot of change ... rather, a lot of evolution! People and organizations didn't stop needing leadership ... they needed it more than ever, but needed it for different things and in a different way. I needed to know what I had to offer, what I would do, what I wouldn't do, understand the needs of others, have a vision, and a plan to apply it the way they could receive it the best. Being willing to tweak content to fit the situation and a concentrated effort to fall in love with the virtual space saved my business, impacted companies, and a brand new virtual and pre-recorded online training series was born and is now a mainstay in my menu of services!

What about personally? Work/Life Harmony matters and it'd be a shame to succeed professionally and hate to return home! The same rules I shared above still apply. Your past with your significant other was epic ... or at least I hope it was! You guys became a couple due to having the right connection at the right time of your lives. Things change and roles change ... you're now seasoned adults, parents, professionals, etc., with life happening and draining you mentally and physically. Remember, the past is gone and you cannot recreate what was; even if you did ... you're different now and it may not feel the same if you intentionally attempt to recreated it. So, take what was good about the past; can you apply any of it to your relationship now and does it make sense to? What could you have fine-tuned from the past ... have you? What's best to scrap and look back on fondly? Who are you now? Who are they? Do you know what your partner needs most from you right now? Apply this as a team and enjoy your evolution. Remember, it's a marathon, not a sprint!

**The Future**

The present is NOW and the future is coming! The change your organization and life have experienced allows you to pivot and evolve! Here are some questions to ask:

1. What do you want things to look like and be like moving forward?

2. Know the vision of those around you! Some of their ideas and dreams will align with yours and the organization ... great! Some will not ... also great! Either marry the two or encourage their vision within your boundaries. You'd be surprised how much more people will do with you, for you, and forgive about change when you apply this!

3. Lastly, whatever vision and plan you've come up with … Be flexible and allow it evolve as necessary!

Evolution isn't something to be feared; rather opportunity to be embraced by realistically examining the past, applying what was learned to the present, and enthusiastically building for the future … Enjoy!

> *"Trying to recreate what was will only take you away from what is and what can be!"*
> – Andre Young

CHAPTER 19

# A Leader's COVID-Effect; How to Keep it Going?

I know ... it sounds weird even to utter the words, keep the effects of a global pandemic going. So many people lost their lives, families lost loved ones, and the world changed forever. This is not to minimize the pain, loss, and suffering of so many; rather an opportunity to live in the positives and manage the negatives ... my life motto! COVID-19 had its negatives, however there's one huge professional positive that's too big to ignore and I implore organizations, leaders, employees, and teams to maintain as we power forward. So, what is it and how do we do it?

COVID forced the professional world into mandatory remote work ... a concept shunned by most leaders before the pandemic. That remote work familiarized everyone with Zoom, Google Meet, Teams, or whatever platform you use. This remote work and consistent virtual meeting format forced us to get human-to-human like never before ... and this is the COVID-Effect! For the first time, employers and employees were going through the same thing, at the same time, and working to figure it out at the same pace ... Wow!

Virtual meetings forced us to exhibit great personal leadership skills by showing up to virtual calls with your head up, eyes up, and smiling! Once you're on that virtual call, it's hard to be inattentive, not have your eyes on who's speaking, and smiling ... as opposed to walking through the office head down and buried in your phone or on your computer, attempting to avoid someone or everyone, and smiling your least.

I once worked at a company and to this day could not pick the CEO out of a police line-up. However, I may be able to identify her by the top of her head; as she walked past me daily with her head down in her phone, no eye contact, and no hello. Be sure this is not you as a leader ... again, you'd be surprised how much more people will do with you, for you, because of you, and forgive about your mistakes as a leader when they feel more connected to you!

Virtual meetings also let leaders and employees into each other's personal lives like never before. In the past, the only way to know the work/life harmony aspect of an employee, boss, or coworker was to see pictures of their family on their desk or meeting their family at the annual company holiday party. The COVID-Effect brought leaders and employees into each other's living room! The fact you could see your boss's significant other walk by, see your employee's kid sit on their lap mid-meeting, hear their dog bark ... or in my case, our pet pig (Hamilton), and hear the UPS guy ringing their doorbell provided an opportunity for us to get more human-to-human than we've ever been.

Through the COVID Pandemic, titles and professional positions at work still mattered; but not as much as getting the job done, being willing and flexible, and EVERYONE on the team exuding great personal leadership daily; outside the watchful eye of corporate management!

So, how do you keep this COVID-EFFECT going for your organization, leaders, employees, and teams in a New Normal?

**Awareness & Planning**

The first thing is to be aware that some of your leaders and employees can't wait to physically come back to work, while others don't want to be there at all ... wishing they still had on their Zoom-Outfit and comfy slippers, and that Frank from down the hall in 2020 may not be the same Frank any longer. In times of massive transition, a lot happens in a day, in a week, and when significant time passes; significant changes are occurring ... Be Mindful!

In times of change and entering your New Normal, don't let "Busy" beat you out of your 1-on-1 Meetings! Many companies around the world have adopted this simple concept, remained consistent, and significantly enhanced morale, motivation, and impact ... it's a true gift for your people, your leadership, and your organization!

**The Human-to-Human Experience**

It's essential to keep the Human-to-Human Experience going! In returning to the office, it's easy to forget the times you saw your boss's or employee's kids on their lap, their dog barking during calls, or that their favorite color is yellow because of the wall behind them on your numerous Virtual Calls. Ask about their pets, partner, kids, and life once you return to the office ... allowing that smile to broaden on their face as they are reminded of what matters most. Of course, not everyone enjoys mixing their professional and personal life; therefore, be mindful of respecting their boundaries and cherishing the fact you were briefly granted access into their private world!

## Allow Evolution

Lastly, allow evolution to occur within your organization, leaders, and employees as the team moves forward! This doesn't mean everyone gets to do what they want, when they want, and how they want ... that's not evolution; that's chaos! Evolution simply means you respect and accept the fact things have changed. What did you enjoy before change occurred, professionally and organizationally, that makes sense to bring back? What did you enjoy or what became most useful through change? What do you want to add moving forward to achieve and evolve the vision of your organization and team? Your Answers + your application of your answers = Evolution!

> *"You'd be surprised how much more people will do with you, for you, because of you, and forgive about your mistakes as a leader when they feel more connected to you!"*
> – Andre Young

# CHAPTER 20

## A Leader's Ear; The Art of Listening to Build Trust!

Hearing is a sense; one of the five senses most of us are born with and take for granted. A few of the simple pleasures I enjoy in life are hearing my kids play together, having coffee outside while listening to the sounds of the morning, or hearing my wife say my name (when she's happy, of course, Lol!) … there's magic in the sense of hearing, and we're unable to turn it off. However, listening is a choice and we have full control of who and what we listen to. Leaders choose to listen to information that leads to evolution and don't mind where the information is coming from. The goal is to listen, apply, improve, and EVOLVE!

Unfortunately, too many times as organizations grow, those in leadership positions listen less and less to those in the middle and on the front-line! This may happen for several reasons: perhaps the company's size has increased the amount of red tape, bureaucracy, and a mess of an org chart. Perhaps it's ego and leaders couldn't imagine a front-line employee having better answers or solutions. Perhaps it's frustration as you're busy and the onslaught of everyone's opinion has become annoying or sounds like constant complaining; which feels like a consistent attack against you and your leadership! I could go on, but you get the point. The truth is ... hearing is a sense, listening is a choice, and as a leader you don't have to come up with all of the answers. Marrying your vision with what your customers/clients need most right now and listening to your employees' ideas to provide the most seamless approach is leadership! So, how do you do the Art of Listening?

**Trust**

TRUST is a big word and the foundation upon which your leadership is built upon. Do your people trust what you say, trust your follow-through, trust you won't hurt their career after sharing undesired or unwanted information, do they trust you to be transparent? You're probably tired of hearing me say this; as I want it to stick in your head ... It's amazing how much more your people will do with you, for you, because of you, and forgive about your mistakes when they trust you and the organization. The opposite is true when trust doesn't exist ... it's incredible how little people will do with you, for you, because of you, and forgive about you when trust is an issue ... Be Mindful!

Trust can be enhanced in three ways:

1.  Manners – I came up with a quote years ago and still live by to this day, "Don't let your evolution elevate your ego!". A please, a thank you, a smile, greeting your people, and email etiquette go a long way! Remember, your manners might be the only positives your people received that day ... and it's coming from their leader. You have no idea what's going on in their home life, their relationship, with

their kids, or the rude interaction they had with a stranger that day!

2. Acceptance of feedback – Whether it's requested or unwanted! For example, some companies send out surveys to gauge where the company is and what employees think. This is supposed to be anonymous; until the boss becomes upset by the feedback and suddenly wants to know WHO said WHAT ... Yes, this really happens in some organizations! Or, someone speaks up in a meeting with an idea, a question, or challenges things and is now blackballed from promotions, targeted, or shunned at work ... Yes, this really happens in some organizations! Or, a Negative Nick or Nancy shares a great idea but is ignored due to their consistent negative disposition.

I've found some of the best solutions to propel a company forward may come from your clients/customers, your front-line people, and even your Negative Nicks and Nancys! It involves you, as a leader, being willing to actively listen to WHAT's being said and WHY it's being said ... rather than focusing on WHO is saying it and HOW they're saying it! We can always go back to address a more professional way to share information. The point is to absorb the gems and apply what's reasonable, doable, and fair into the process of things.

When I worked in a Mental Health Facility, our building was shut down due to Black Mold. The company planned to build a brand-new building and it was an exciting time! My coworkers and I were eager for the new digs and believed, as a staff, we would have some input on the design; such as ideas concerning placement of classrooms, Behavior Pods, and offices to allow optimum flow for emergencies situations. Well, no one ever asked and the building was constructed. We were all bummed; as it would have felt quite exhilarating to be a part of building something we'd use daily. Although it was nice to have a new building and we made it work; the layout proved to be somewhat dysfunctional and caused its growing share of problems throughout my tenure.

When I started what has now morphed into my business, I was a poor listener. I had my ideas, consulted no one, and rolled out new ideas and expected smiles ... boy I was wrong! I remember designing a t-shirt with the company name on it and underneath read, "of Reading, Pa". During the unveiling, a friend and member said, "Why does it say of Reading, Pa. I don't live there and what if you want to expand?". I remember my smile turning into immediate frustration and shutting him down quickly ... all the while, knowing he was right, it was a good idea, it would have been best to collaborate first, and the shirt would have been better with less writing on it. A rookie mistake, not to be made again ... and this leads us to point number 3!

3. A.F.E. – After Feedback Engagement! – This is of monumental importance. As a leader, how do you respond to your people, your team, and the idea after hearing feedback you don't enjoy and when the consensus is against you?

**Ask**

This is simple, short, and sweet. You want to enhance your leadership and listening? ASK your people their thoughts and don't penalize them for sharing. Whether it's your employees, employer, team, spouse, or kids; Share the issue, then ask your question. It may sound like, "I have an idea about _____. I'd like to know what you like about it and what would you fine-tune or change?". It allows the person to say something good about your idea first, removes your ego, and invites theirs in. This doesn't mean every idea will be fulfilled, rather ideas will be listened to... and this leads us into Follow Through!

### Follow-Through

To intentionally ASK and not DO tends to ruffle feathers. Therefore, use the third rule in my Leader's 3 and share the fact one of three things will happen when ideas are shared:

1. You go with their idea; as it was so great it blew your socks off!
2. You collaborate on the idea because there's a bigger picture the person may not know about.
3. You don't do their idea as your vision and vision factors are currently directed elsewhere and make the person aware of the bigger picture; challenging them to fit their idea more appropriately into the Vision Factors.

The final point of Follow-Through is to DO SOMETHING about the information you received. Whether it's a positive conversation about the idea, applying the idea, explaining why it's not the idea's time, or sharing that the implementation of the great idea is outside of your control. I hope you enjoy your new ears; as listening is an art form that will enhance not only your Leadership & Work/Life Harmony but also that of those you're leading!

*"Some of the best solutions to propel the company forward will come from your clients/customers, your front-line people, and even your Negative Nicks and Nancys ... Be Mindful!"*

– Andre Young

# CHAPTER 21

# A Leader's Fun; The 4 Keys to Creating & Maintaining Fun at Work!

Fun ... even the hint of the word creates tingles of anticipation and excitement! However, as time passes and things change, so can our definition of fun; leaving you feeling lost, empty, and stuck on auto-pilot. My definition of "Fun" changed from my teenage years to my 20's, from my 20's to my 30's, from my 30's to 40's, and I'm sure it will continue to evolve. A few of the most perplexing times of my life have been when I no longer knew my definition of "Fun", professionally or personally. You may be so busy being busy with your head down and blinders on chasing that singular definition of "Success" that when you look up you're unaware of what "Fun" is. So, how to enhance fun at work; impacting not only your leadership but for your people and teams?

## Brainstorm

I share a Leadership Question through my App (YEN PUSH) once per week and recently I posted … "What's your current definition of "Fun" professionally? In your personal life? Do you know your people's answer? Your significant other's answer? Your kid's?" What a thought-provoking question … and whatever your answer and theirs … what a powerful thing for you to know!

As a leader, being curious enough to ask these questions and knowing the answers of your people will significantly impact your leadership and their work/life harmony; allowing you to brainstorm ideas for activity, impact, and traditions!

*Activity* – This can be defined as the brainstormed ideas from you, the leadership team, and employees that occur spontaneously or are repeated throughout the year. It may be that Pizza Day your team is so fond of, impromptu staff outings, or staff meetings offsite. I once had a boss walk into the office and spontaneously say, "Let's have our morning meeting at the café down the street; my treat … ROAD TRIP!". You would have thought she was handing out $1,000 bills and we all just won the Super Bowl!!!

*Impact* – These are activities purposefully meant to be of impact and value in the lives of team members either professionally, personally, or both! Perhaps you decide to bring in a Motivational Speaker, provide various trainings, spontaneous call-outs of praise to acknowledge those on your team who've achieved professional goals, earned an incentive, or experienced a great personal achievement!

*Traditions* – Sometimes, a brainstormed Impact Activity becomes SOOOO much more! The shout-out of praise becomes something that occurs once per month or grows into a huge annual event for your organization. Perhaps it's something smaller; like that much needed and well-earned Happy Hour that now occurs every Friday or once per month. Whatever it is … it's now important, expected, and synonymous with your team and the company. Organizations, just like families, benefit from traditions … something meaningful, expected, and cherished that brings people together for a common purpose. Be mindful, some employees may grit their teeth about the tradition and the process it demands, but tend to be the same people to complain if it would stop. Follow Through with your traditions and let them evolve as necessary!

My favorite tradition I've had the honor of being involved with as an employee happened entirely by accident! I was a Mental Health Worker in an Alternative School for youth struggling emotionally, behaviorally, and with their mental health. On the last day of school, all staff lined up on both sides of the hallway to dismiss the students one bus at a time. The first classroom was dismissed and as the students walked down the hallway with teachers, staff, and counselors on both sides … staff began to clap, cheer, say the students' names, give high-fives, and it became a cheering gauntlet of love and positivity! To our surprise, we never saw the students smile so big, try to hide their smiles, and some almost bursting with pride. It dawned on me … this may have been the first time many of the students had ever been applauded for, were made to feel accomplished, or special. I'm proud to say this became a powerful and fun-filled tradition that I hope is still happening today!

### Follow-Through

Whether the "Fun" you create for your team is Activity, Impact, or becomes Tradition … Be sure to FOLLOW THROUGH! With the chaotic pace of the day, the quarter, the year, and the projects … it's easy to get caught being busy. Too busy to remember that "Fun Thing" that doesn't rank up there in the importance of meeting metrics, having meetings, and maintaining customer satisfaction. I've found, what gets scheduled gets done. Whether it's a meeting, a task, or "Fun" … be sure to put it in your calendar, your team's calendar, and the organization's calendar and have some FUN!

## Upgrade

You've followed-through and have done a wonderful job of providing "Fun" at work … Now, it's time to upgrade the experience. Doing something once may be great, twice is good, three times is ok, by the fourth, it could get freakin boring! When you aren't focused on upgrading the experience as a leader; you may find yourself flying into Burnoutville and Frustratedtown as you begin to hear your team complaining, "This same thing again" or looking as if they'd rather be doing anything else anywhere else. Be mindful of gifting your people with an upgraded experience over time and to include their suggestions into the idea vault!

## Enjoy

This is imperative! It would be a shame to plan "Fun", follow-through, and upgrade only to be miserable throughout the process. Enjoy the impact of gifting your team and organization a great experience. This isn't to say the process of "Fun" isn't taxing; as the behind-the-scenes of any amusement park is packed with hard-working, diligent, and exhausted staff.

As a leader, be mindful to nurse yourself to protect from burnout, know what to delegate and who to delegate it to (possibly creating a "Fun" Committee), or potentially utilizing companies or consultants specializing in event planning (www.blueboard.com). This, mixed with your consistent personal leadership of showing up daily with your head up, eyes up, smiling, greeting, doing your best, and being your best will allow you to better enjoy the "Fun" along with everyone else!

You may be asking yourself … "How can we do fun when we're working remotely?". This is an excellent question with many answers. Some ideas I've seen, some I've done, and others I'm sure you, your team, and consultants can brainstorm.

One company sent each of their team members gift baskets with treats to be enjoyed during their virtual meetings. Another company sent Happy Hour Gift Baskets to be enjoyed for a Virtual Happy Hour. I have a rule of screens up and be willing to unmute during my Virtual Leadership Trainings and utilize group air-claps as an applause when attendees share their P.O.W. (Positive of the Week). Most employees will not return home, enter their office, or turn on their computer to a standing ovation … never underestimate the power of applause! There are many more ways to have "Fun" when physically at work or virtually and I implore you and your team to get to brainstorming!

*"Don't be so busy being busy that you, your team, and the organization forgets to follow through on having fun at work!"*
– Andre Young

# CHAPTER 22

A Leader's Butt-Kicking; How to Take a
Butt-Kicking When You Thought Your
Were Right or Knew You Were Wrong!

During my Speaking Engagements and Trainings for organizations, I often share with leaders how to have the tough conversations with their people; because when they're not willing to ... I guarantee they won't be leading for long. However, they're two sides to every coin; what's the best way to RECEIVE the tough conversation? The truth is, whether you're the CEO, a Supervisor, or Front-Line Employee ... no one is exempt from being on the receiving end of the tough conversation for mistakes made. Front-Line Employees may receive this butt-kicking from supervisors, while supervisors receive it from their bosses, and CEOs may have a Board to answer to! So, how do you best take a butt-kicking when you thought you were right ... or knew you were wrong and get called out?

I must preface, I refer to a professional butt-kicking as being confronted by a leader about a mistake you made that may involve a conversation and/or professional consequence such as a tough and questioning conversation, a write-up, suspension, etc. Let me be clear ... Verbal abuse and obviously physical abuse are ever warranted or to be tolerated!

With that said, I can clearly remember my three biggest professional butt-kickings. The first was my senior year of college as a football player. It was Summer Camp and we were in the middle of two-a-days. Practices were over for the day and I was headed to the final meeting of the evening. It started at 8:00pm. My watch said 8:00; however my coach's watch must have said 8:01pm. I entered the room with everyone already present and him addressing the team. Upon entering and being the only one standing ... this man lit into me like I've never been talked to before in my life and kicked me out of the meeting! I still don't have the words to describe what I was feeling at the moment. All I know is, I've been 15 minutes early to everything since 1998, Lol!

My second Butt-Kicking came during my first job after college. I worked in a Residential Mental Health Treatment Facility and was scheduled to attend a court hearing for a Resident. I entered work upbeat and ready for the workday like any other day and my boss asked what I was doing on the Unit. Apparently, I was supposed to be at court! I completely missed it and had no real reason as to why ... it simply slipped my mind. The next day I came to work and checked my schedule, it was the dreaded 1:00pm – 11:00pm shift for seven days straight! I saw it, looked at my supervisor, he looked at me, we both nodded, and all was understood ... and I never missed another court date again!

My last butt-kicking came as I was burning out of a job. I thought I'd retire from that job, but fell out of love with the organization, the changes, leadership, and everything that came with it ... and it showed! I was more disconnected, vented inappropriately, and severely behind on my paperwork. When my boss and his boss addressed this with me ... I said and did some of the concepts below:

**A Leader's Listen!**

Remember, hearing is sense ... Listening is a choice! Of course, you want your boss or coworkers to deliver a tough conversation to you in the perfect way; the way you prefer to hear and wrapped in a pretty bow that won't hurt your feelings or offend you. Or, perhaps you'd rather them say nothing to you at all! I train leaders in organizations worldwide on how to initiate the conversation, using your top two Languages from my Leader's 7 and more. The truth is ... more people haven't received my training than have and your bosses delivery may not be as nice as you'd like ... or think you deserve.

The first thing to do is realize most bosses would prefer not to have this conversation with you! Most likely, they didn't wake up wanting to ruin your day, they may be more anxious than you to have the conversation, and honestly would prefer the job was done correctly so they can focus on the other 15 million other things that require their attention. So, whether you thought you were right or knew you were wrong ... be mindful of your face, your posture, and be open to learning something new when the Butt-Kicking comes knocking.

As an employee, Be mindful to make eye contact, but not the glaring "I'm going to flatten your tires in the parking lot later stare". Nod your head, affirming this is a serious conversation you are interested in having. Be mindful of your posture. It may be easy to close off as you look down, away, continuing to work while they're talking, crossing your arms, tapping your foot, legs shaking, etc. Instead, keep a comfortable Covid-Distance, stand at a 45-degree angle with your hands comfortably at your side or in your pockets. If you're sitting; be mindful to sit up straight instead of slouching and disappearing into your seat.

Lastly, be open to learning something new from the conversation! Some people are all guns blazing because someone or anyone dared to confront them about their mistakes, behaviors, and observed patterns. Leaders see confrontation as an opportunity ... to learn, grow, and evolve. What can you learn from this conversation? What will you apply to ensure you become an asset and not a liability moving forward? These are simple things to add to your toolbox as you evolve as a leader!

### A Leader's Validity

This is short, sweet, and important! What are they right about?

My coach was right about me being late. My boss was right about me missing the court date. My boss was right about me being behind majorly in my paperwork and becoming a cog in the system due to my disconnectedness and negativity. It doesn't mean your boss's tactics of handling the conversation were the best or something you must tolerate ... only you can decide that. The point is to first seek validity of what they are right about and accept full responsibility for it. This leads us to the next step!

### A Leader's Coaching

Often is the case, your boss may be right; however, you may be right too! Therefore, it's not about right and wrong ... it's about evolution. How do we evolve a conversation and allow for professional and organizational growth? The truth is, sometimes you have to make your leaders lead you and make your coaches coach you!

Get over the "Shoulds" of my supervisor should know the answer, they should know how to do … , they should…. they should, they should, just because they make a little bit more money than you and have a title? Please remember, leaders are people too, they make mistakes, and most were promoted because they excelled at one thing … not because they were great at leading people. Therefore, help your leader to lead you!

When it was brought to my attention my paperwork was behind and my attitude had changed; the truth was I was behind because every time I left my office to get lunch, go to the copy machine, or simply make my rounds I ended up assisting in ten restraints. I struggled due to changes in leadership as the company brought in a manager that was incompetent to the job and created numerous safety risks for clients and staff. The organization also accepted any and every client into the facility; and our staff was not prepared or built for this new way of doing things.

When helping the leader to lead you, the trick is to select an issue you actually have control over, present a suggested solution, and ask for help. For me it was … "You are absolutely right. I'm drowning in my paperwork and I wish I would have come to you before you had to come to me. It's on me and I thought I could catch up. The truth is, years ago I was able to bring work home to stay afloat. My kids are older now and my time after work is different and I'm not able or willing to do work in the evening after my kids go to bed. It's also difficult to catch up here as we're constantly in crisis mode due to new clients we're accepting and the current staff we have. Whenever I leave my office, various crises pull me away, and at this point I'm not sure what to do or how to prioritize it all. I have two ideas: get my paperwork done right after sessions and create a time designated to paperwork scheduled in my daily calendar ... what do you think and is there anything you'd fine-tune?".

Their response was something I didn't expect ... they listened and then offered two weeks at headquarters to fully catch up. Although the bigger issues were still present; I was heard, was able to stop drowning, and brought attention to the bigger picture. After listening and seeking validity, you may have to make your leaders lead by sharing your list, sharing an idea, asking for fine-tuning, and seeing what happens. You'll learn a lot from their response ... for better or worse!

**A Leader's Thank You!**

Leaders close conversations ... especially the difficult ones by thanking the other person for having it with them! When you're the one receiving the Butt-Kicking, "Thank you for bringing this to my attention. I'm sure you have a ton of things to do and I want to be great here; so I appreciate getting better from this. This will no longer be an issue on my part". Feel free to make this Thank You Statement your own ... as long as you mean it! When you're the one giving the professional butt-kicking ... thank the person you're giving it to for taking it!

I can still hear my college coach yelling my name every 10 minutes at every practice. It got to the point I went to speak with him and asked, "Why are you on me so tough?". I'll never forget his response, "The day I stop yelling at you is the day you need to start worrying". Wow! For him, the day he stopped yelling was the day he didn't believe you could get any better and it no longer mattered. I still talk to him and thank him to this day!

Remember, no one is exempt from a professional butt-kicking ... from a boss, an employee, a customer. When it's your turn ... be sure your face and posture are right, seek validity; what are they right about, help them to lead you, and as hard as it may be ... thank them for the opportunity to evolve; as they would prefer everything to be going smoothly and not to have the conversation in the first place!

> *"Thank the person you're giving the Butt-Kicking to for taking it ... and ... Thank the person providing the Butt-Kicking for caring enough about you, the team, and the organization to give it."*
>
> – Andre Young

# CHAPTER 23

# A Leader's "Squozen"; How to lead through the squeeze of leadership!

I'll never forget a former boss of mine walking into the office in a frazzled state, rattling off a bunch of conversations to herself aloud, suddenly looking at me, and exclaiming, "I feel squozen!" … Yes, she made up a word and I knew exactly what she meant and how she felt … and I'm sure you do too! She was a recent new hire to the organization with a wealth of experience and skills, but ill-informed of the inner-workings and day-to-day pace of chaos the job entailed … it didn't help that Senior Management and her boss were in offices miles away and out of touch with how the job had evolved. Leaders may also feel squeezed as they must meet the demands and metrics set by Senior Management while caring for, protecting, impacting, and influencing their team working on the front line. So, how does Middle Management lead when feeling "Squozen"?

**Understand Your "Squozen"**

The first thing to do is to get a better understanding of your stress. Are you stressed because the situation is new and par for the course of leadership? Many times, when you feel "Squozen" as a leader … your people tend to feel the sam … and may react in not so professional of ways: negative talk, outbursts, absentee-ism, gossip, etc. Here's an important question … Are you feeling "Squozen" and your people aren't … due to your poor delegation, lack of trust in your staff, your people have simply checked-out, or have never really checked-in? I could go on, but you get the point. There can be a plethora of reasons for your "Squozen"; find out what it is and develop a plan for what to do about it!

**Request 1-on-1's**

Now that you better understand your "Squozen", it's time to request 1-on-1 Meetings. I share the importance of leaders having 1-on-1 Meetings with their people and how to do it. In this case, as the leader, I'm suggesting you request monthly 1-on-1's with your boss. I know … you're busy and so are they … so what! The meeting doesn't have to be long and the point is to share the positives, maintain high standards, address concerns, and to limit surprises. You will also learn a lot about your boss (and possibly the organization) in how they respond to the request. Remember … some bosses will and some bosses won't. Be mindful to request your 1-on-1 via email; as leaders protect themselves with proof of asking for guidance, assistance, and leadership!

When sharing this with Senior Management, the 1-on-1 bullet points are the same from Chapter 9:

- P.O.W – Positive of the Week/Month
- What would you like to get out of our meeting today?
- Meshing Goals

- The Plan
- What was your Biggest Takeaway from our meeting?

However, as a leader, when you're requesting the meeting, the flow may change a bit to:
- Start with the professional positive/s since the last meeting
- Is there anything you/the organization needs more from me ... and/or my team right now?
- Share a current concern ... when you have one? Remember to be prepared with a suggested solution; asking what he/she likes about your idea and anything they'd fine-tune. This helps to enhance your leadership and learn the bigger picture you may not be aware of!
- The Plan

These meetings are a powerful way to share your "Squozen" with higher-ups without sounding like you can't handle the tasks or are constantly complaining ... enhancing your leadership, your boss's, and that of your team. Be mindful to email your boss afterward to Thank them and confirm the plan in Black & White. A conversation that's not documented, didn't happen ... and they will also appreciate the Thank You ... Boss's don't get many of those!

### Gather & Rally

The 1-on-1's with your boss will provide you a look behind the curtain ... some things you will like and others you won't. After receiving feedback and increased clarity ... share it with your people in the 1-on-1's you've scheduled with them or in a group meeting. Great leaders are transparent with information and are sure to smile when delivering news; focusing on the positives of how it will benefit employees, customers, and the organization as a whole.

### Request Training

Many who feel "Squozen" are so busy treading water, they don't realize they're in quicksand ... the more you do the more you sink ... and if you're not sinking professionally; you may be sinking in your work/life harmony! This seems like an odd time to request a training, right? Wrong! This may be a perfect time to enhance your leadership and processes for you and/or your team.

I've worked in places where the leader may attend a training (getting some well-needed knowledge and break from the office) with the expectation to share the information with the team upon their return. I've worked in other places where employees took turns attending trainings and returned to teach it. However you choose, please remember, when you're putting off being "Better" due to being "Busy" ... "Busy" isn't going anywhere and doesn't plan to stop. YOU must choose to be a nerd about your craft; enhancing your training ... as everyone will revert to their highest level of training in times of change, crisis, and "Busy" ... Be Mindful!

### Networking & Self-Care

A "Squozen" Leader will only be a great leader for so long! Therefore, networking and self-care are a necessity ... not a luxury. Enhance your leadership and work/life harmony by networking with professional peers and at level above within your organization, at networking events held in your community, and on social media. There are wonderful people out there interested in meeting, conversing, and potentially adding value to your life professionally and sometimes personally.

I met one of my most recent best friends at a Networking Event several years back. It was like being in kindergarten again ... there was something about his energy and professionalism; we were in entirely different fields, planned to meet for coffee, and have been friends since! We even do business with each other from time to time while our kids play with one another! Sounds cheesy, I know ... but there are millions of stories just like this ... why not you?

I can talk for days about self-care and in my books and trainings I do! Eventually, being "Squozen" at work will leak into your conversations at home, your relationship, and how you engage with your kids and friends. Remember ... what you think about and talk about all day will leak into your behaviors ... and then your consequences ... positive or negative. Be mindful to make YOU a priority! Know what you need to take care of yourself and who to do it with ... The Negative Nicks and Nancy's, energy-drainers, and complainers in your life, professionally and personally, are not the ones to hang out with. As a leader, you wouldn't build your professional team with these individuals ... why allow it your personal life?

*"Great leaders are transparent with information and are sure to put on a smile when delivering news; focusing on the positives of how it will benefit employees, customers, and the organization as a whole"*
– Andre Young

# CHAPTER 24

## A Leader's Upgrade; How to Upgrade Your Team, Your Leadership, Goals, & Success!

Upgrade ... What a word! Some people attach "upgrade" to their ego and material things such as their car, their house, clothes, or even their partner. Others may be anxious or fearful to upgrade and neglect the process all together; as it will depend on them or their people learning new things ... slowly turning them into dinosaurs. Dinosaurs can usually be detected as you hear them saying, "This is the way we've always done it"'. In contrast, leaders recognize not only the benefit of upgrading ... but what to upgrade and how to do it. As a leader, upgrading is imperative for you, your team, your organization, and your vision!

Upgrading, by my definition, is the act of implementing new strategies, systems, or people to your vision that takes your goals to the next level more reasonably and efficiently ... increasing your reach and your revenue ... at the same time decreasing your sweat equity. That's a mouthful, but one of the truest things I've ever written!

Let's think about it ... As a leader, any upgrade you make to personnel or technology would only be worth it if the person or the technology increases the efficiency of an existing process and/ or impacts revenue. The new person or technology may initially increase your sweat equity as you may invest time and funds to introduce the new upgarde: provide training on how to best use the new upgrade and of course, your 1-on-1 Meetings to evaluate the benefits of the new upgrade. However, in the long run ... your willingness to upgrade will provide you more time to focus on Evolving Acts ... those acts that will take your company into the future and best care for your people and customers in the process!

Before we continue, it's necessary to clarify the difference between upgrading technology and upgrading people on your team. Technology doesn't have feelings and has no choice in whether to work for you or not. As quickly as technology advances, your upgrades must keep pace to keep you and your team in the race. Technology doesn't care which program you use, if they're replaced, how you lead, or how they will feed themselves and their family. Your people do!

Before you decide to upgrade by making changes to your staff, be sure you've done your job as a leader:

- Bringing in people that are not only qualified but also best fit your desired culture
- You've connected regularly with your people with A Leader's 1-on-1 Meetings and you've made it an expectation the leaders within your organization will follow through with their 1-on-1's with their people.

- You operate not only as a boss, but also as a coach … providing information, tools, trainings, and opportunity for your people to upgrade themselves.
- Lastly, you give your people the power and authority to do the upgrade without micromanaging.

When you've done this and things are still an issue … it may be time to upgrade your personnel, but how to do it?

### Invest

Any upgrade will cost you something … "Better" usually does! As a leader, you must be willing to spend more of your time, your energy, your money, or all three. My goal heading into 2021 was to upgrade my networking process and passive income strategy; focusing on my books and prerecorded online leadership training program.

Over the past few years, I really enjoyed reaching out to each and every person via social media. It felt more personal to do it myself and I hope they felt my sincerity as I asked to connect, share my content, and later we got to officially meet and speak! However, the more speaking engagements and trainings I presented worldwide, the less time I had to network the way I wanted … a great problem to have! Therefore, upgrading my personnel and technology to add a Virtual Assistant and a Contact Specialist became essential. To do it correctly, I had to invest my energy and finances into searching for the best system (for me), training an Assistant, and interviewing a Specialist. So, there's the financial and energy investment!

My focus on increasing Passive Income also led me to develop a Pre-Recorded Online Leadership Program. I enjoy everything I get to do; however, I can't deny the process of creating the online program was tremendously tedious, to say the least! My point is ... A Leader's Upgrade will start with an investment of your time, energy, and possibly your money. Be sure to spend your time clarifying your vision, your energy coaching your people, and your money on the best system or program for everyone ... not just one department!

## Ramp-Up

You and your team must decide what you do "Great". Does it refer to your product? Your client's reaction to it? Revenue generated? Goals met? Or, all of the above? If things are going "Great" ... does it make sense to upgrade its reach? Can you handle more work, orders, etc.? If so ... put your process on steroids and GO!!!

What's going "good" in your business and on your team? How could you best ramp it up ... making it a bit better. You and your team must decide what "Better" is. My favorite question to ask is, "What do you like about _____ and what would you fine-tune?" ... Ramp-up by marrying your vision with their feedback!

## Hold or Stop

Just as some things are going "Great" and "Good" ... some things at a standstill. This can be for several reasons; it could be a bad idea, not attractive to customers/clients, little time and energy invested into the project, lack of passion from your team, limited buy-in from the company, funding, etc. Now is the time to evaluate to either hold or stop.

Not everything needs to move forward or needs an upgrade. Some projects or ideas are best put on hold until more time, energy, or money can be properly invested. Other ideas are best to be stopped and scrapped! It doesn't mean the idea can't be revisited or fined-tuned; it simply means everything doesn't need to happen right now! This is a golden rule of Leadership & Work/Life Harmony: Just because you can, doesn't mean you should.

Too many times, well-intended new leaders have a bunch of great ideas ... but unknowingly put themselves and their team on the path to burn-out as they attempt to do everything all at once. Here's a tip ... out of all the ideas, projects, and things you'd like to attack ... what are the Top 1,2, or 3 that would make the biggest impact for your organization and customer/client base? Why? What's the best way to proceed in that direction RIGHT NOW; breaking it down into smaller steps? This is your focus ... then move on to the next. Be sure to clarify the New Vision & Vision Factors, Expectations, and Rules of your Upgrades with your team, and enjoy your evolution!

> *"Be sure to spend your time clarifying your vision, your energy coaching your people, and your money on the best system or program for everyone ... not just one department"*
> – Andre Young

## CHAPTER 25

# A Leader's K.N.O.W.; How to KNOW What You Know and Develop a Process!

You wake in the morning, get ready for your workday, arrive at your company or laptop, work a full day, return home and repeat ... taking for granted all of the things, big and small, you've effortlessly accomplished in a day! Whether you're a Front-Line Employee, Manager, or the CEO ... it never ceases to amaze me just how much we get done in a day and it stems from how much we know ... without even knowing that we know!

You may currently be on auto-pilot getting your job done daily, however when you look closely ... you know a lot about your job, how the organization wants you to do things, how you may actually do them that works best, who to talk to get certain things done, and how best to follow through. This process you've created serves you and can help your coworkers, your team, your company, and possibly the world! I recently spoke with a gentleman that now helps companies develop processes and strategies as his own business and he said, "When I was an employee, I didn't know what I knew until I said it aloud and wrote it down".

I was very similar … when I was a Mental Health Therapist, it was seemingly easy for me to come up with Group Therapy ideas, concepts to discuss and utilize, ways to communicate, and I struggled to understand why it wasn't as seamless for others. In positions of leadership, I found it easy and fun to determine a vision and the steps necessary to achieve it. Now, as a business owner and Leadership Trainer my job is to know what I know and break it down into common-sense, easy-to-apply, digestible concepts to allow for a professional and personal evolution … and you can too! So, how do you do a Leader's K.N.O.W. and develop your process to be of impact?

### K. – KNOW What You Know!

This part is most difficult because sometimes we are truly are unaware of what we know and that others don't. My youngest son plays quarterback and has played the position seemingly since birth. It's been 7 years and counting, how many practices, games, and private coaching … I'm proud to say, he's very good at what he does! One week he was unable to practice, his backup was hurt, and the third-string quarterback saddled up. It's the same position, they're the same age, the same plays, and the same coach … but the results were quite different. My son began to share with his teammate his process of how he prepares, the smallest of details of footwork, hips, shoulder positioning, and all that goes into throwing. He had no idea how much he knew … until he had to show someone and say it aloud.

My questions for you are … At your job, what are you great at? How do you do it? Imagine you're getting promoted, but the only way you can accept the position is to train your replacement.

Say aloud what they need to know, who they need to know, what they need to do, and how to do it. You may be surprised by the depth of your knowledge and plan.

### N. – Number Your Steps

This step is short, simple, and sweet. Once you KNOW what you know, say it aloud, and write it down ... put them into steps and number them. Now you have an official process that can be easily understood and replicated! Think of the articles or videos that catch your eye as you scroll social media, but furthermore the ones that entice you to read or listen further because of the steps mentioned ... 4 Easy Steps to ... 5 Ways to ... 3 Simple Ways to ... You get the point! Be sure to number your steps, keep that number low, be clear and concise in your directions, and use language a 13-year-old can understand!

### O. – Be Obsessed

The word obsessed used to make me cringe; until I understood that everyone that's great at something tends to be obsessed with it! Michael Jordan was obsessed with basketball and winning. I love all music and Hip-Hop is my favorite, Lil-Wayne is obsessed with creating. I'm obsessed with my craft of Leadership & Work/Life Harmony. The point is, obsession can be a virtue ... as long as your obsession includes these three intangibles:

1. Diligence – Develop your process, know your process, and obsess over your diligence toward your process! Consistency will take you farther than motivation!

2. Production – At the end of the day ... leadership, success, and your K.N.O.W. will come down to production! Does your process produce desired results and beyond? Become

obsessed with production and watch how many doors open for you!

3. Evolution – Most processes will need to evolve to survive and thrive through times of organizational change. As a leader, be willing to evolve your K.N.O.W. as necessary!

**W. – Winning Culture!**

Does your K.N.O.W. make your organization better? Your peers better? Your boss better? These are simple, yet essential questions to ask and answer…as some people's K.N.O.W. are simply short-cuts that short-change the organization and their professional aspirations. So, how do you know if your K.N.O.W. is the bad kind? It only serves YOU; as you get tasks done faster and short-cutting things … you also experience a lack of professional growth, development, and opportunities.

A brief side note: I often share with organizations and leaders the importance of getting their "New & Unknown" Employees around their "Inspired & Motivated" Employees as quickly as humanly possible for two reasons. One, people and new employees tend to stay with the group they initially meet. If that's the "Inspired & Motivated", great! If that's the "Grouches" and "Short-Cutters", not so great! Two, new employees like to do what they were initially trained to do … they learn, they do, and habits are formed. It's really difficult to break habits six months to a year later in their annual review … That's not leadership!

Be sure your K.N.O.W. works to create winning concepts professionally for you, your team, the company, and also…. your customer and client base! Know your K.N.O.W., enjoy your K.N.O.W., share your K.N.O.W., and who knows … maybe one day YOUR K.N.O.W. will create your own brand and business!

*"Develop your process, know your process, and obsess over your diligence toward your process! Consistency will take you farther than motivation!"*

– Andre Young

A Leader's Production

*Leadership comes down to results ...
and results come down to processes!*

# CHAPTER 26

# A Leader's 30; The First Month Leading Your New Team!

To me, there's nothing worse than a Dream-Killer … I have a few pet peeves and this one ranks pretty high on my list! I once played on a team, trained all off-season, was in the best physical and mental shape of my life and on the first meeting of camp … the coach enters and says, "No one in here is going to the NFL, so….". I don't remember anything after that. Although I wasn't deterred from my dream, I was stuck on how a person in leadership could start a meeting with brand new people that way … and expect unbridled trust and loyalty. Another time, I took my son to his first day of football camp and the first thing the coaches mentioned was, "statistically only blah, blah, blah make it to the NFL and you're one injury away from…". Another time, I remember a new CEO coming to visit our facility. She was ushered around like the President by seemingly four bodyguards, made minimal eye contact, gave the politician smile and wave, and left the building. What was that!

When you're in a professional position of leadership, at some point, you'll have your first experience walking into your new building, meeting your team, and leading those who want to be led, don't want to be led, and those that could care less about being led ... not to mention finding your flow, the process of how things work, who really holds the power ... and where the bathroom is, Lol! So, what to do? Let's explore a few things to do over your first 30 days to get you started!

Before we officially jump into the 4 Key Points ... it makes sense to ALWAYS, in the beginning, throughout the middle, and at the end of your tenure to walk in with your head up, eyes up, smiling, and greeting people! Remember, some people may have heard of you, haven't at all, or may hate your guts because you took THEIR promotion! Be sure to make and maintain a positive and approachable demeanor that exudes the same energy you're going to want your staff to display on a daily basis.

**Gather!**

Get your team together as quickly as you can! They know you're coming, hopefully ... and everyone may be a bit anxious. When possible, it may be great to meet with whoever hired you; gathering any last-minute details, changes, and/or employee updates you'd benefit from knowing. Hopefully, those that hired you have set a scheduled meeting to introduce you to the organization or your team. As a Professional Speaker, it's always nice to be introduced! It takes a bit of pressure off me, and I gain the professional endorsement of someone the audience knows and hopefully respects (the trick is to keep the introduction positive, upbeat, short, and without wordy organizational jargon).

When this isn't the case, your people may be in flux with their own meetings and daily fires to put out ... plan an Introduction Meeting for later in the day or treat to lunch. This meeting proves to be interesting as you stand to speak and intorduce yourself. It will also be interesting viewing the faces in the crowd ... who's genuinely excited, interested, bored, agitated, and those that don't attend.

This is the time to have one of the most important conversations you must be willing to have as a leader ... and it goes like:

1. Hello and introduce yourself ... I always like saying, "Happy Monday (or whatever day it is)!". You'd be surprised how many smiles and giggles you get. Perhaps you bundle your positives, professionally and personally, sharing what company you're coming from, that you're happy to be here now, and if you're comfortable sharing personal info do so ... perhaps you're a proud mother or father of 3, just got a new puppy, or just became a grandparent. It's incredible who you may bond with or who may bond with you when you eliminate the jargon that no one really cares about and share real-life positives; allowing a human-to-human connection!

2. Thank your new team for their hard work and effort up to this point. Even if you're walking into the worst team ever with the worse morale ever ... the fact you're walking into a job means the organization still lives and something was done right. Sometimes, the only positive you can find is that the team is breathing ... and for now ... that has to be enough; celebrate it!

3. Make them aware of what's great about the team, their effort, and how it's contributed to the organization's bigger

picture. In addition, you're excited to use this as a springboard to where WE are going next!

4. Share that the team and organization will continue to do great and is excited to fine-tune, add, and possibly subtract some things to become elite. We are going to be "THEE _____!" and although I have ideas, I don't think it'd be fair to start anything until I've met with each of you individually (or at least your direct reports), as teams, and attend a few team meetings. Thanks so much for having me and I'm excited to start this process! I always like to end with, "Let's be great and have some fun!". This leads us into the next Key!

**Not Now & Observe!**

So many times, as the new leader, we enter with our ideas of how things should and need to be. Even though you may be right, it may prove to discount some of the good that's been accomplished. When I was newly promoted, I managed before I knew how to lead … wanting everyone to be like me, think like me, have my superpower, and care as much as I did about whatever I cared about … completely missing the mark of my team, what they've been through, enjoyed about the job, disliked about the job, their experience with past bosses, and what they wanted to get out of working for the company. I wish I would've done what I'm about to share with you.

During your first 30 days (or fewer or a bit more; depending on the size of your team) you're gathering nuts like a Leader Squirrel. Winter is coming when you re-meet with your staff to institute changes … and at that time, connections will matter!

During this 30 Day Period:

1. Schedule 1-on-1 Meetings with your people and don't cancel or reschedule … and please feel free to address some of the questions I just shared in this chapter or use my Leader's 1-on-1 format from earlier in the book. When using The Leader's 1-on-1 Meetings for the first time, it may be a great idea to share the format and timeframe of the meeting with the attendee to help decrease their anxiety and to ensure a great first encounter! To quickly recap:

   - P.O.W. – their Positive of the Week … You go first; allowing them time to think; as you provide an example of what to say.
   - Then, what would they like to get out of the meeting?
   - How long they've worked here?
   - What do they like most about the job?
   - What's the most frustrating part of their job … and be honest?
   - What did they liked about their last boss?
   - What are they or the team struggling with?
   - What's their vision is for themselves professionally … and potentially help them with their Vision Factors!
   - What do WE need to be focused on to become and stay elite … as a team, as an organization, and for your customers.
   - Share what you expect and need out of the attendee and team to be elite.
   - End by thanking them and asking, "What was your biggest takeaway from our meeting today?". Their answer to this question is a juggernaut as they walk out of your office or leave the virtual call feeling like they got something out of it; rather than YOU telling them what was good about the meeting … Be Mindful!

2. Attend and Observe team meetings. This is not the time for your input; rather a time for observation. How does your team engage with one another? An employee may be great meeting with you alone, but observing how they engage with their team, in meetings, and in real-time is different! How do they listen to the ideas of others, make decisions, delegate, and how do they receive feedback?

3. Meet with your leaders individually to review what they think is great about their team meetings and what they'd like to fine-tune to become elite. This is also the time to address the positives you witnessed associated with the running and results of their meetings ... along with tips to help fine-tune!

**Gather Again!**

It's been about 30 days ... now it's time to get everyone together again! During this regather, it's time to share what you observed was great and address the additions and/or subtractions that will be made to move the team and organization forward to elite status ... be sure you have a simple and working definition of what YOU mean by ELITE!

I've shared The Leader's 3 throughout A leader's Toolbox and it's time for it again as it's one of the most important and necessary tools you have as a leader:

1. Share your Vision for your team/organization. The premature leader stops there ... What are the Vision Factors? The 3-5 things that when your people/team do them consistently, the Vision takes care of itself!

2. Expectations - What are your expectations for your people/team/ organization as a leader. Mine are the 3P's: Be Positive, Passionate, & Productive ... which correlates to

no gossip, being sure to exchange pleasantries with others, no lewd jokes, living in the positive and managing the negatives, producing at an elite level, and providing elite service to customers, clients, and coworkers!

3. Rules – What are the new rules to best move things from bad to good, good to great, or great to elite? I suggest no more than three. Feel free to use mine:

- Be on time; preferably five minutes before you said you'd be somewhere!
- After 3-4 emails about the same thing, let's get on a call to work it out!
- Please accompany your problem with a suggested solution; allowing your people to elevate their leadership skills, think outside the box, and protect your time. You now have options to go with their idea, collaborate to fine-tune their idea, challenge them to fit their idea into the bigger picture and Vision Factors, or not go with the idea; as it's not viable or the desired direction of the organization.

**Meeting with Your Team/s!**

Sharing your Leader's 3 with the big group is a logical start, but it's like getting together the company to share the mission statement one time. It's simply a start, not a process that takes you anywhere. Your personal leadership in how you carry yourself, enter the building, connect with your people, and follow-through on your Leader's 3 will always set the tone and provide an active model for all to see!

Re-meet with your team of leaders, as a group, to drive your Leader's 3 home! Remember … you observed team meetings, you've been meeting 1-on-1 with individuals, and have met with the leaders to applaud and fine-tune. This is the time to meet with leaders to develop and fine-tune their own Leader's 3 for their teams. Everyone's Leader's 3 does not have to match yours, but they must all align and it's YOUR job to make sure that's the case!

There goes your 30-Day Plan (give or take a few days/weeks depending on the size of your team and organization). It's a lot; as leadership is not for the faint of heart. You know, like I know, this is easier to read than to do ... and at some point, your people will show themselves, for better and for worse. Reward those who choose to stay on the train and accept that not everyone who starts with you GETS to finish with you ... and that's going to have to be ok. Enjoy the journey!

> *"As a leader, an employee may be great meeting with you alone, but observing how they engage with their team, in meetings, and in real-time is different ... Be mindful and observe!"*
> – Andre Young

# CHAPTER 27

## A Leader's Message; The 2 Key Points of Presenting to Your People!

So, being a professional speaker isn't your full-time job ... it is mine, and it's critical you connect in the beginning, share the meat of the middle, and recap at the end. As a leader, you will stand up often in front of your team and organization to give a speech, share information, or introdcude something or someone ... and have all of the anxieties that come with it; as public speaking is the biggest fear for most people!

I've had the pain and privilege of being on both sides ... listening to forgettable speeches from a new leader sounding like a politician, speaking all about themselves, or rambling on in a monotone voice to the point I'd rather pay them to stop than to hear one more word! I've also made the mistake of being promoted and not addressing my team at all; leaving everyone to the expectation that nothing had changed. So, how do you do it?

## The Focus

Truthfully, it makes me cringe every time someone calls me a Motivational Speaker. I know it's the language they know best of how to describe what I do. However, in my mind, I picture a speaker rah-rahing you up … and when you wake up the next day all energized but don't know what the heck to do! If someone needs to call me a motivational anything … I'd prefer a "Motivational Teacher". I mention this because you, as a leader, are your organization's and team's new teacher, mentor … and Motivational Teacher. You may not speak with the passion and skill-set of a professional speaker yet … here are a few speaking tips to put in your Leader's Toolbox!

First, let's discuss what not to do! When addressing their group, most leaders use too many words to say something simple. Believe me, simple can be better and can always be fleshed out more later when people have questions at the end or meet with you 1-on-1. One of my pet peeves from college was professors requiring students to write 20-page term papers … What and Why!!! Can you imagine receiving a 20-page work email from someone? Or you asking a question and someone rattling on for 20 minutes straight with an answer? My wife works in law and I certainly understand some jobs and situations may require a hefty stack of paperwork … but not always and defiantly not in your initial meeting with your team! Be mindful not to use so many words and remember a sign of social intelligence is being able to say a lot in a little!

Second, eliminate the bureaucratic jargon! I'm honored to meet with extraordinary leaders around the world and often ask them to tell me about their company and what they'd like to get out of bringing someone like me in? Some leaders, not many … but some will begin down this path of professional jargon-filled and a doctoral level-vocabulary rant; leaving me befuddled, frustrated, and confused. I know I heard them, I know what each word means, however the barrage of words is so unnecessary and if I feel this way ... what do their people feel like?

Although, you as a leader, may be right with everything you said ... the massive jargon-dump also works to dehumanize you and can further disconnect you from your people. There may be a time and place for your organization's jargon; simply be mindful of who you're speaking with, when the jargon is necessary and appropriate, the glazed-over eyes of the people you're speaking with, and simply speak human-to-human ... being willing to fill in more when needed or requested. I operate off a simple rule; if your 13-year-old can't understand it... it may be too convoluted. It's incredible how much more people will do for you, with you, because of you, and forgive about your leadership mistakes when they feel a connection with you ... and it starts here!

Third, make your message more real! Facts and plans only go so far ... to make them more impactful, include stories. The stories can be about you in positive or negative professional situations, about previous coworkers (not sharing real names of course), or even stories that are happening within the company now but changing names, gender, and the company to share a problem, solution, and outcome ... without directly calling people out. This is a great way to backdoor a real issue and not confront anyone directly on your big day. You'll be surprised who may come up to you afterward and say, "Wow, that really hit me; I felt you were talking just to me.". Stories make YOU more real, your plan more exciting, and your connection more solid as other leaders can relate and some employees are more intrigued!

**How to Do It?**

We explored the things to eliminate and what to add, but how do you DO IT when it's time to speak?

**Greet**

Greet everyone and Thank Them for letting you have their time!

**Welcome**

Welcome them to what you'll be talking about today. Keep it short and to the point; allowing them to know the topic and what to anticipate

**Who**

Who are you and what do you stand for? As a Keynote Speaker at conferences, I usually greet, Welcome (saying the name of my presentation), then my name and area of impact ... I'm Andre Young, professional speaker, author, leadership trainer, and founder of You Evolving Now and my mission and impact is enhancing two things ... Leadership & Work/life Harmony!

**Explain Your Impact**

Why are the things you're mentioning so important ... and why is it important for them? This is a perfect time for a story about how doing things the new way has worked great in your experience or how doing things the wrong way negatively impacted those served, the company, and employees. Share your Vision, the importance of it, and how it benefits them professionally and personally!

**What to Do & How to Do It!**

As I mentioned in the previous chapter, if this is your first-ever meeting with your new team or organization ... it may be wise to say, " I have ideas, but I think it'd be unfair to start or stop anything until I've met for 1-on-1's with everyone (or Direct Reports) and attended team meetings to get the lay of the land first. I look forward to our next meeting to come back together!".

Otherwise, it's The Leader's 3 time again! Now that you've eliminated unnecessary words and jargon, greeted and welcomed everyone, introduced yourself, added stories, and explained your impact ... it's time to share your Vision & Vision Factors, Expectations, and Rules related to whatever plan you're introducing. I mean to be redundant with The Leader's 3, because it's that important and is a fantastic preface statement. Your people will not be able to deny they've heard it; making it easier for them to incorporate it into their mindset and daily acts ... and easier for you to reward those on board or have the tough conversations with those who aren't!

This process may not make you a world-renowned professional speaker, but it certainly won't make you any worse! Enjoy sharing your message with your team and being a leader you can be proud of and your people need.

*"As a presenter, sharing stories make YOU more real, your plan more exciting, and your connection more solid as other leaders can relate and some employees are more intrigued!"*
– Andre Young

# CHAPTER 28

# A Leader's Delegation; The 3 BIG Wins of Delegating and How to Do It?

Delegating responsibilities would appear to be a logical part of leadership; and in theory it is, however in actual practice it can be a sticking point for many of those in leadership positions. Some leaders like the job they were initially hired to do and choose to nobly stay in the weeds with their team. Some believe no one can do the job like them and will inevitably mess it up; therefore it's best they do it all. Others wear their "Badge of Busy" with pride and ego of how much they can do. While other leaders are uncomfortable delegating all together. Or, believe it or not ... are being bullied by their employees. Yes, this is a real thing! While conducting a Leadership Training, I'll never forget a C-Suite Executive asked, "If I say or delegate _____, what if they say _____(insert rude/sarcastic/unprofessional comment)__ back to me?". This shocked me for several reasons ... My first thought was how comfortable their staff must be to make such a snappy and rude comment. My second thought was, how do they still have a job here? So, why do we need to delegate, what are the wins of delegating, and how do we do it?

### The 3 BIG Wins of Delegating

1. Delegating allows leaders to build other leaders. Remember, Mangers focus on tasks ... while leaders focus on the people that do the tasks! It may feel good and personally rewarding to know as much as you know, do as much as you do, and to be depended on so heavily; however when the ship sinks every time you walk away, take a vacation, or attempt to enjoy life outside of work ... THAT'S NOT LEADERSHIP and will eventually lead to burnout!

   - In my early days working in a Mental Health Facility, I was the superstar! I could relate to everyone and anyone, manage the day-to-day, deescalate any crisis (big or small), and there were days I entered the building with staff removing my jacket and taking my briefcase as I went into "Emergency Mr. Fix-It Mode". This period of my professional life was pumping my ego, but not my leadership! What would happen if I took the day off? It would have certainly been more chaotic for the team and facility, but the world wouldn't have stopped spinning. My staff and yours would still be at work, dealing, and managing.

   - It was time to evolve and teach what I knew, understand my team's individual superpowers, step back, and let it get uncomfortable for a while ... for them and for me! This allowed my staff and coworkers to become more confident in their leadership and skillsets. I quickly passed this message to every "Allstar

Worker" that came after me. Leaders know when to step back, why to step back, how to step back, and when to step back in!

2. Delegating allows leaders to reduce their workload. Crisis, promotion, and retirement will always show us just how busy we really are. When crisis strikes, professionally or personally, look at all of the busy work and minute details you struggle to maintain and have to catch up on. When you want to get promoted … it's hard to move on when you haven't trained your successor and the company needs you to stay where you are because you're the only one that knows what to do and how to do it. Or, when you want to retire but the company or team would flop if you left right now. I could go on, but you get the point! Delegating will allow you to lighten your load; allowing for growth and evolution for both you and the organization!

3. Lastly, delegation allows you to move up or move on in peace! This is simple yet powerful. Moving on to your next professional endeavor or retiring in peace knowing you left the organization, your employees, and team better than you met them and ready for their future is priceless!

### How to do it?

I've found there are four things all leaders can do to best delegate:

1. When it's time to delegate projects off your plate, it's imperative to know "What" you're giving away. Be sure to explain the project to your employee or team; as well as your expectations of what success looks like. Remember, you've been doing this task for months, years, maybe even decades … it may be brand new to them!

- This is a perfect time for what I call, A Leader's Book-Ending. Too often, leaders delegate projects and then disappear, assuming their employees know what to do or will figure it out ... only for the employee to be ripped into later for doing a poor job. When delegating a task or project: share what the project is, why you're delegating it, and ask, "What are you excited about regarding _____?", "What, if anything, are you anxious about or have questions about?", determine what constitutes an emergency regarding the project, and share with your employee the best way to contact you with any questions or concerns they may have throughout the process. When the project is complete, book-end your leadership by asking, "What did you enjoy most about the project?", "What was your Biggest Takeaway or lesson learned?", "What would you share with someone else coming up behind you to do the same task next year?". These questions allow your people to fully digest the experience, to know what they know, and enhance their skills to teach it to someone else in the future ... That's leadership!

2. "Who" are you giving the delegated task to? Does their superpower align with the task? Are they familiar with the task? Do they need training? Will you or someone else provide the training? Are they able to make the process their own while you white-knuckle the experience of letting things dip before they springboard to success?

3. "Why" are you delegating the task away? Giving a task away simply to give it away is not leadership. Knowing your "Why" is leadership. What do you hope to get out of the task or the individual ... and do they know your

answer? This leads us to one of the most important concepts of delegation...

4. The Evolving Act! Here's a leadership truth ... when you delegate tasks away and don't have a bigger idea to work on ... you'll eventually roll up your sleeves to jump back in to micro-manage and annoy the heck out of your people and team! With the time you've gained by delegating effectively, your Evolving Act is the "Bigger Vision Work" you're ready to focus on to best propel the organization and your team forward!

As a leader, delegation is not only necessary; it's an art form and will include following through with your 1-on-1 Meetings, knowing your people's top two professional languages (The Leader's 7), and delegation will become a whole lot easier!

> *"Moving on to your next endeavor or retiring in peace knowing you left the organization, your employees, and team better than you met them and ready for their future is priceless"*
> – Andre Young

# CHAPTER 29

## A Leader's Pass-Off; Grooming and Introducing Your Replacement!

Years ago, I outsourced a part of my business and we've worked together for years to create a successful process. Recently, there was a situation that required immediate attention. Upon calling and calling, I couldn't get in touch, and when I finally did … due to their busy season, I was rushed off the phone and passed-off to a gentleman who was supposed to be more of an expert, had the time, and would be happy to help. All of this may have been true … but didn't wipe away the yucky feeling I had of being discarded, passed-off, and having to start over with someone I didn't know or trust. Sound familiar? Either you've been there or you're in a leadership role and may have inadvertently done the same thing due to massive growth, transition, or simply "Being Busy.".

Before my business evolved and it became what it is today, it was on college campuses and just beginning to enter the corporate world; back then, I was a piece of the puzzle. I had You Evolving Now Dreamleaders; experts in their own fields of fitness, real estate, and finance; all focused on enhancing work/life harmony for employees. However, when it was time to pass-off from me to my Dreamleaders ... the colleges and companies wanted me! As a leader, you may be in this same situation where you've been promoted, business has grown, changed, things have gotten busy, and it's time to delegate and pass-off. So, how do you do it ... without creating that yucky feeling for your client or customer and that yucky feeling for your people of not being wanted or able to measure up to you?

**Validate!**

Who's the person you have in mind to pass-off a task, client, or customer to? This is an important question because the answer cannot be just anyone! Do they have the expertise and skill set? Are they new or newish and require more training and experience? Do they want the position or opportunity? It would be a shame to pass-off someone that doesn't have the skill-set or has the skills but doesn't wish to do it. When someone is passionate about their purpose and helping others, it shows; making their mistakes or lack of knowledge easier to forgive and patience more abundant! Lastly, what's their vision in taking over for you? You may be surprised at what they say!

**Grooming!**

As a leader, grooming is your responsibility! Be sure your people are equipped with the necessary knowledge, tools, and training to be the best for both the organization and the client/customer. When passing-off and grooming, you can't help your people's age or experience level, however you have control over who you're inviting into your team, knowing their vision, helping to enhance their skill level, and maintaining high standards and expectations!

**The Pass-Off!**

The Pass-Off isn't meant to be this one-time magical moment, "Hi this is _____. He/She is going to be working with you from now on. Bye!". That would be awful! Or even worse, "I'll have _____ reach out to you. They're taking over for me". Or the dreaded, "I've moved on or am swamped right now, I'll have _____ reach out to you." What is that!!!

The Pass-Off is best to happen gradually, especially when you know it may eventually be necessary. As a leader, invite the employee or coworker into current meetings with the client/customer. Begin by introducing them, who they are, what they do, and why they're there. Candid is best ... "We have great people and leaders here. We want to be sure they get as much experience as possible; getting to meet our clients/customers so as we grow, our people can move up without creating chaos within the company or for you. ____(Employee's Name)____ will most likely take over for me at some point and will be in charge of your account and business.". As meetings progress, The Pass-Off Person is more included in conversations, shares ideas, then eventually leads the meetings, you begin the leave halfway through, then BAM ... the meetings and the client are theirs. This is the long process when needed. You know your people, client/customer, and business to make necessary alterations to best lead!

When I was a Mental Health Therapist I started every new session with the same series of questions to make it easier for my clients ... and for me! What brings you in? What would you like to get out of working with someone like me? Have you been in therapy before? What did you like about it or the therapist?

What didn't you like? This is how I work ... let's marry the two! When starting new work with a client/customer recently passed off to you, these are some great questions for you. When you're the employee or coworker receiving the client/customer, here's an important question to set you up for success. "I know you've worked with _____ for a while and they're great! I want to create an awesome experience for you, what did you like about working with _____? Anything you'd like to fine-tune or add to the process as we move forward? This is how I like to work _____ and I'm excited to get started!" Their answers will give you a blueprint for how to excel. Simply listen, apply, and do ... as long as it's legal, doable, fair, and within your organizational and work/life harmony guidelines!

**Be Available!**

Passing-Off is not your last step as a leader! Remember, this may still be new for your people and you still know the client best. BE AVAILABLE to answer questions, emails, and texts pertaining to the pass-off. This keeps the train on the tracks and moving smoothly!

The "Be Available" process may be frustrating for you as you thought you were done and moved on to the other 7,000 things on your list. Therefore, it may make sense to schedule a regular meeting time to briefly discuss Pass-Off-related issues. This meeting allows a designated time for non-emergency questions, follow-ups, and ideas to ensure your organization, team, and people stay elite in their service and customer/client satisfaction! Enjoy your Leader's Pass-Off and your evolution!!!

*"As a leader, grooming is your responsibility! Be sure your people are equipped with the necessary knowledge, tools, and training to be their best for the organization and the client/customer"*

– Andre Young

# CHAPTER 30

## A Leader's Doorway; 4 Keys to Maintain the Harmony of Your "Open Door" Policy!

You've been there as a leader, you're working in your office and someone knocks at your doorway with a question ... a simple question that could take two minutes turns into an hour-long conversation you didn't plan on having! This process happens two more times with colleagues and BAM ... there's half your day! This was my kryptonite as a new leader; I was a Connector Type and loved to engage and converse ... and my office quickly became the hang-out spot for questions and conversation. Initially, I enjoyed it ... until I found myself bringing work home, falling massively behind, and my superiors eventually having the "Tough Conversation" with me as to why my work wasn't done. Although there were other factors regarding the timeliness of my work ... the lack of leadership of "My Doorway" was a big one! To be fair, this is a delicate issue of harmony; when your door is always closed ... you're a disconnected leader. When your door is always open, you're always available for the perceived emergencies of others.

Also, through the Covid Pandemic, the reduced immediate access to people sparked the need to have scheduled Virtual Meetings ... which helped to increase patience a bit; as people had to WAIT for you to get back to them and proved the sky would not fall! So, what to do to protect your doorway and find the sweet spot of harmony in this area; enhancing your leadership and that of those on your team?

**Time-Frame It!**

Two types of people will want to cross the threshold of your doorway, the employees and coworkers you enjoy and the ones you don't ... those are the ones with a poor attitude, gossiping, seeking the easy answer instead of refining their skills, etc. No matter your feeling, be a leader and time-frame the interaction. It may sound southing like, "Hi _____, do you have a minute? What can I do for you? They will share their dilemma ... or the fact they just stopped by to chat. "Ok, just to let you know, I'm middle of something right now so I have about 5 or 10 minutes and I have to get back to it ... how can I help?".

This statement is something I wish I'd implemented earlier in my career as a leader and it certainly made an impact when I did. The hardest person I found to do it with was the employees and coworkers I enjoyed because it took significant personal leadership on my part to end a fun conversation and get back to task. This may also be difficult for leaders who have the urge to please or find it difficult to set boundaries. I've discovered "Time-Frame It" keeps you polite, willing, addresses the issue, and works to protect your time.... as long as you follow through and end the conversation at the time you allotted. This will also prevent your employees and coworkers from saying you were dismissive and disconnected … Be Mindful!

**The Meeting!**

When "Time-Frame It" is successful, you can stop there and your professional world is golden! When it doesn't … and you have more and more people visiting your office for 5-10 min slots that take over your entire day … something is wrong! You fixing everyone's problem is not leadership and they are not exhibiting leadership by always asking you! Therefore, it's time to protect yourself and request a meeting with your direct supervisor (unless you're the Big Boss). Please remember, your boss may feel the same way about their doorway. So, follow my rule of accompanying your problem with a suggested solution, explain your plan for how you will attack the issue of your doorway with your team or individual, ask what he/she likes about it and if there's anything they'd fine-tune, and request a timeframe of three weeks to a month to see how it works.

Now your higher-ups understand there's a problem, that you actually desire to do your work, you're willing to lead your team, you've worked to develop a plan, did not throw any of your people under the bus to make yourself look better or them worse … and you now have their backing and support if and when there's an issue or complaint that goes over your head!

Perhaps your plan of adjustment is for your team or an individual … we'll get to that in a bit. Perhaps the plan is for YOU … a more flexible work schedule to arrive earlier or later in the day to get work done, leave earlier or later to get work done, or to have a regularly scheduled time of day or day of the week with your door closed to get the most important parts of your job done.

Many years ago, I chose the latter ... closing my door at certain times of the day significantly limited the travel across my doorway. However, beware ... as it can become addictive and you may soon find yourself disconnected from your people and the real-world happenings of your team and the organization! I also selected Friday afternoons as the day to complete my more monotonous tasks outside of my office in somewhat of a common area to be in the mix, making myself available, and to see the day in real-time. When you choose this option, be mindful of the day ... when a crisis takes over on a Friday ... that work then piles on to your next week, and the next week, and so on! Pick a day that works for you, your team, and the organization.

**Your People!**

It's time to be transparent with your people or team! This can be uncomfortable to share ... as you really enjoy your team! You can do this in a group or 1-on-1. The goal is to share things will look different moving forward; as there's a new expectation focused on enhancing your leadership, theirs, and working more effectively as a team. Your door will be closed during set times to allow for _____ and that emergencies are defined as _____. It never ceases to amaze me what people may consider an emergency ... usually, a mess up on their part constitutes an emergency for you to fix RIGHT NOW! Through the pandemic, team members had to schedule a Zoom Call or wait for an email response. Suddenly, because your office is ten steps away ... everything is NOW and takes an hour to discuss and solve?

Meeting with your people is not only about sharing the changes that meets your needs. It's also to understand why they have so many questions, don't know what to do, how to do it, and why they're living in your office. There are many possible reasons

… So many new employees are working remotely that have never physically shaken hands with leaders, existing employees, or new hires. Perhaps there's been monumental turnover and they're unfamiliar with processes. Perhaps, due to an employee shortage the company simply hired available bodies. Maybe through transition, proper trainings were not administered and everyone's attempting to figure it out on the fly. Or, an employee is actively trying to get fired or the boss's cousin! Whatever the reason … be sure to understand why they need so much from you and work to develop a plan that enhances their ability and their leadership!

**Follow Through!**

It would be a shame to go through all of this and not follow through! I know things are busy … and "Busy" has beaten more people, professionally and personally, out of "Better" than anything else in the world! There will be time when crisis, deadlines, and other significant circumstances arise and all-hands-on-deck are necessary … however, that's not every day! Therefore, follow through with your plan and fine-tune it as necessary from the smallest strategy of "Time Frame It" to the biggest of "The Meeting" and "Your People" … OR, keep getting what you're getting, set up a turn-style at your doorway, and stop complaining!

*"You fixing everyone's problem is not leadership and your people aren't exhibiting leadership skills by always asking you without providing a suggested solution … Be Mindful!"*
– Andre Young

# CHAPTER 31

# A Leader's Solution; How to give "The Answer"!

We discussed protecting your doorway and having your people brainstorm a suggested solution before coming to you in the previous chapter. However, there will be times when your people will get stuck and simply don't know what to do. Or worse, they make in-the-moment decisions with great professional intent and are later chastised and reprimanded into never making another decision again! As a leader, sometimes you will simply have to give "The Answer" ... the answer for how to fix something, how to do the process correctly, or the answer for how to do it right the next time!

As an employee years ago, I worked in an Alternative School. It was its second year open, the staff was new, and we ran the roost as all corporate higher-ups were located at headquarters. A rule established by the higher-ups was if a student left the building, they were not allowed back in under any circumstance ... and to make that point very clear to every student. Of course, the day came when two teenagers decided to exit the building. My partner and I shared the rule of no-return-entry beforehand ... and about an hour later the two young men returned, knocking at the door with "Big Gulps" asking to reenter the building. My partner and I maintained protocol, as we were trained to do; but also we had no idea what was in the containers and didn't want to endanger students or staff by allowing two potentially intoxicated students back into the building. Long story short ... a week later, our "BIG Boss" from headquarters came to pay my partner and I a visit and read us the riot act regarding our decision.

When we explained we were following protocol and made decisions based on the safety of others ... we followed our statements up with ... "What would you have preferred us to do and what would you like us to do next time?". I still remember the silence that ensued and the puzzled look on our boss's face. NO ANSWER and complete confusion. My partner and I were not our best professionally that day as we exploded in frustration for being beat down and provided no answer on how to do it better or A NEW WAY!

On the other side of the coin, I've been a leader and had the honor of working with well-intended employees that simply didn't know what to do when THEIR way stopped being effective. This is not the time to chastise, berate, or demand "Better work". Remember, most employees want to do a great ... or at least good ... and when they're tapped out of ideas, they need answers from YOU as their leader! So, how to do it?

### Address the Issue

This is an important first step ... be mindful to address the issue, not the person! When you let your feelings about the person get in the way of improving the issue it will negatively impact your leadership ... and theirs! Remember, as a leader, you care about everyone, but you may not enjoy everyone and everyone may not enjoy you ... and that's OK.

Here are a few questions to ponder before engaging with your employee ... or to discuss with your employee: What's the issue? What was done well? What needs to be fine-tuned due to unforeseen issues?

In the story I shared, it would have been great for our boss to say "I understand we had an issue here with two students leaving the building. I know our policy is not to let them back in; things have changed and we can be liable if something would have happed to them. You guys did great at explaining the rules to the gentlemen beforehand and ensuring the safety of others when they returned. We will not be able to continue this process moving forward and we have to come up with something that legally protects us, protects those that leave our care, and the students in the building. I'm thinking this_____ and would like your input and thoughts because this has to happen fast as the situation could happen again in the next two minutes and we MUST and WILL be prepared." Approached this way, it would have been hard for my partner and I to have an issue, and would have been more than happy to be a part of the solution! This way sounds nice and ideal for employees, but life isn't always that way. Perhaps a new policy has already been approved ... this would be a great time to applaud great employee effort, share the new way, the why, and the how.

**Seek Understanding**

Whatever the issue causing you to become involved and provide a solution is massively important. Remember, what doesn't get addressed gets repeated! WHY are the mistakes continuously happening? Perhaps this is how the person has always done it and thinks they're good at it! I've been there ... praised for my work; then switched organizations to find their standards were higher and I wasn't as great as I thought. Perhaps, they don't have the training or tools to be successful and a broken machine or poor WIFI are causing the issue. Or, maybe they don't care and are content doing the bare minimum. In any case ... seek understanding of the "Real Problem" with the intent to help them fix it moving forward. "Fixing it" may come in various forms ... making yourself available to meet and coach, organizing on-site trainings, funding off-site trainings, and/or shadowing opportunities for staff. Get creative and marry what you want your people to improve in with what they need most and the best way to give it ... and it's hard to lose!

### The Evolving Question!

Here's a powerful question to ask before providing your solution ... "If you had it to do over again, what would you do differently?". It's amazing what people say! Sometimes, this question will provide the solution or possible pieces of the solution moving forward.

When I was in graduate school, my assignment was to complete a transcript. I had to tape a 10-minute portion of a therapy session with a client, type everything I said, their response, my response, and an alternative response. Although I hated every minute of typing; it was a life-impacting experience! What a life-changing lesson for anyone, professionally or personally! It forced me to be more mindful of every word I uttered ... and more importantly, trained me to Stop/Think/ and lead with my Alternate Response instead.

**Solution Ready**

After you've addressed the issue, sought understanding, asked the Evolving Question ... and they have been unable to develop a workable solution; it's your job to be Solution Ready with "The Answer" of what to do, how to do it, the benefit!

When you're unable to come up with a solution on the spot and time permits ... be human enough to say you don't have an answer right now, would like more time to think, and provide a timeframe in which you will get back to them. Use this time to either brainstorm your own, ask your leadership peers or a mentor for advice, or research ... whatever you do ... come up with something, honor the timeframe you provided, and give your solution; allowing "The Answer" to evolve over time and as necessary!

When you deliver the solution, take the shakiness out of your voice and say it with confidence, assertiveness, and own it! Too often, leaders present the solution timidly or apologetically. Share the new way, why it's good for the organization and an expectation for everyone to be All In ... doing their best and being their best in the process!

Enjoy the journey of caring for your people, your organization, and developing leaders ... it's an amazing experience and sometimes YOU as a leader will need to put your leadership on display as you provide "The Answer" ... and now you know how!

*"What doesn't get addressed gets repeated ... Be Mindful!"*
– Andre Young

# CHAPTER 32

A Leader's Hybrid Magic; 4 Ways to Lead in a Hybrid Work Environment!

The Covid-19 Pandemic created an epic shift in how employers and employees viewed the workplace; bringing forth a "New Normal" called The Hybrid Workstyle! Many small companies and entrepreneurs ... including myself ... were operating this way Pre-Covid, but very few large companies with the amount of staff to consider, daily change, ever-evolving regulations, and do-more-with-less expectations Covid created.

Hats off to companies, leaders, employees, and teams that trailblazed a new path; however, it comes at a price ... everything does! It's great to be able to work from home, wear your Zoom-Attire, see your kids more, have your significant other working in the other room, and any other positives you can think of. The concern is ... you're home most of the time, seeing your kids more, your significant other more ... Lol ... have gotten used to pajama bottoms, the email drip never turns off, some employees don't want to return to the office, and how the heck do you establish cohesiveness and connection when everyone is in and out of the office at different times! A Leader's Hybrid Magic is two-fold as leadership is a Two-Way street … Leaders must do their part; and so must employees! So, how do you do it?

### Do & Be

Do & Be refers to your choice, as a leader, to show up daily to the office, your Virtual Calls, and your 100th email of the day DOING your best and BEING your best! Remember, be big on The 3P's; Positive, Passionate, and Productive? One without the other two is incomplete! As a leader, it's our job to model this on a consistent basis. I know it's impossible to do it all the time as you're a human being and are possibly burning out, tired, frustrated, and don't like or agree with current changes … all the while having to deliver the news to your team with a smile!

BEING your best also has a lot to do with your face and body language. I once had a boss that entered the office every day looking as if someone woke him up at gunpoint, dragged him out of bed, and into the office to do his job. Upon seeing this daily, I remember thinking … "Is this what a promotion makes you look like around here? No Thank You!" and "If this is what leadership allows and accepts … No Thank You!".

As an employee, no matter where you are in the company or your title … you can be a leader when you choose to be! Leaders must deliver their message to you with a smile. However, you live in the real-world muck of the frontline after the message is delivered and the boss walks away or clicks off the Virtual Call. You have a choice … go converse or call your coworkers to begin the bashing of how stupid everything and everyone is … making your disdain for your job compound day after day, month after month, year after year. Or, Do and Be your best ... marrying what you want to do and give with what the team and organization currently need most from you right now; becoming an asset instead of a liability to be dealt with later ... Be Mindful!

## Collaborate

Hybrid work schedules have made collaboration even more important; and some would say a job all of its own! I know you're busy, however you cannot be so busy you fail to inform and stay connected with your people. Gone are the days of walking down the hallway to run something by someone. Be intentional regarding your collaboration with your peers and employees ... designating time to collaborate. I had the honor of speaking with a company that built a brand new building focused on Hybrid Magic. Although it's a work building, no employee is expected to be there daily unless they desire to. The building is almost like a resort and the leaders only bring their people in to intentionally collaborate, celebrate, or congregate ... Wow!

## The Information Highway

Emails and texts aren't going anywhere and I'm sure you're flooded with them throughout the day and possibly the evening. As a leader, it's necessary to inform your people ... it's also necessary to help your people best prioritize; as everything cannot be a High Priority/Handle Now Issue. The scariest and saddest thing is when EVERYTHING is High Priority/Handle Now Issue and your people consistently come through ... leadership may feel no need to address the chaotic-pace, flawed process, and eventual burn-out. Therefore ... Chaos & Crisis becomes the culture rather than order, procedure, and follow-through ... and due to Hybrid

Work, you may not be able to see your people's physical, emotional, and mental stress.

How do your staff prefer to receive information from you? Since your people may not be in the office, it may make sense to share what an "Emergency" is and collaborate on a best way to communicate it? Recently, I was emailing my Assistant twenty-plus emails per day. After experiencing a few misses, I evaluated the process. I brainstormed why the misses could have happened, asked her thoughts to improve the process, proposed an alternative system of chunking emails, and she stated she was fine with how things were and shared adjustments she'd make to ensure no further misses. We agreed things would stay the same with one addition ... when she emails someone on my behalf and they fail to respond ... she will automatically reach out 48 hours later to say hello and follow-up! Collaborating on the Information Highway is critical to your leadership and ability to stay Positive, Passionate, and Productive!

Lastly, Hybrid Working Schedules mean your 1-on-1 Meetings are more important than they've ever been! In Hybrid Working Environments, I'd suggest Virtual 1-on-1's. When you're people come into the office, they're eager to get stuff done and it's already hard as so many employees know they're in that day and waiting to pounce! Let them reacclimate themselves to the office, lead through those issues, and get stuffed crossed off their list they had planned for their only day in the building!

**Team-Building**

How do you create, maintain, and inspire cohesion when everyone is everywhere, busy with everything, or no longer wants to get together with each other? The answer is the dreaded Team-Building Activities! I don't mean the cheesy games an instructor would have you do that has nothing to do with your job. I'm suggesting:

1. A set and mandatory day your team is in the office. Those working remotely or too far away attend the meeting virtually.
2. Scheduled Happy-Hour Events for the team or organization (Live or Virtual with gift packages)
3. Celebration Events to celebrate successful project completion, promotions, organizational milestones, birthdays, etc.
4. Activity Retreats: Bowling, Family Fun Centers, Bean-Bag Toss Tournaments, Breakfast Meetings, Lunch Meetings, and so much more!

These are a few ideas and I'm sure you can think of more; asking your coworkers what they'd enjoy or feel free to google ideas. As a leader, please know … you will not make everyone happy! The Grouches, Negative Nicks & Nancys, and even some of your Inspired & Motivated will complain for their own reasons … simply being grouchy or that they're too busy to be there. The point is togetherness and connection.

Years ago, one of my favorite things to do at networking events was "Speed Networking" … just like speed dating but professionally. It was done in the beginning and was a great way to get to know everyone; leading to a more comfortable event afterward. There were long tables and those sitting on one side of the table never moved; while the other side slid down one seat after three minutes. It was a lot of fun and the trick was to have pre-set questions ready to be asked. Here are a few I've brainstormed:

"What do you do here and what do you like most about your job?"

"What did you do this summer for fun?"

"What professional highlight are you most proud of?"

"I will ... _____ "

When I did my first and only You Evolving Now Conference years ago ... instead of putting names on the attendee's nametag, the nametag read "I will..._____" and they had to fill out the rest. It was amazing the things people wrote. One gentleman I knew for a while wrote "I Will ... become a racecar driver" and we had a great discussion about his passion and plans. I never knew that about him and to this day, I don't remember his name, but I'll never forget his dream ... and now I know what to talk to him about when I see him again! It also allows you to best connect your people, coworkers, and leaders by their similar passions!

As an employee, you're a leader too! Be sure to attend these planned functions as your best self, DOING your best, and BEING your best. Remember, there was a team of people or a person that spent a lot of time organizing the event and you'd appreciate someone not crapping all over your effort ... Be Mindful!

### Give Credit

This one is simple, with so many of your people working remotely and in a hybrid fashion ... compliments go a long way! Thank your employees ... and your leaders ... for their effort, their successes, their attention to detail ... and be sure to send your "Give Credit" email or text during working hours. The appropriate timing of your compliments keeps their anxiety low as their phone is not ringing, dinging, or chiming off-work hours. It also respects their intimate relationships ... so their phone isn't buzzing while they're lying in bed having to explain why their coworker or boss is messaging them late at night about how great they are ... just saying ... Be Mindful!

*"Collaborating on the Information Highway is critical to your leadership and ability to stay Positive, Passionate, and Productive!"*

– Andre Young

# CHAPTER 33

## A Leader's Quota; The Pros, Concerns, and 2 W's!

Ibelieve most things have their positives and negatives; I prefer focusing on maximizing the positives and managing the concerns! Quotas within a business are no different; whether you like them or loathe them they have their positives and concerns. So, what are they and how can you enhance your Leadership & Work/ Life Harmony and that of your people?

**The Positive**

Quotas set forth by an organization or leader provide a standard and an expectation of what's to be achieved. It may address how many calls to make in a day, how much must be sold in a month, etc. Whatever the quota is ... your people and teams are all aware and on the same page!

Leadership is displayed when the quota is examined further:

1. Is the quota set reasonable, doable, and fair for the people doing it and the circumstances of the time? Selling out all of the hotel rooms during a global pandemic may not be the most reasonable, doable, and fair quota to set and hold your people accountable to.

2. This doesn't mean we scrap the quota altogether; rather you adjust, become creative, and let the quota evolve as necessary. Perhaps the number set for the quota stays the same, but additional time is allowed. The number stays the same, but you decide to expand your geographical reach. The number may decrease as you develop more creative ways to serve. Throughout COVID, it was difficult for restaurant owners to stay open let alone meet their quota to break even. They became creative in altering their service to take-out, pick-up, and outside dining. This altered their quota number as well as added a new stream of revenue once their previous way of serving returned.

3. Do your people have the tools to be successful in achieving the Quota? This is a simple yet powerful question and ignored by too many organizations. Your people are willing … and most employees want to do a great job, hit that number, and be rewarded for it in return! However, that darn machine is old, faulty, and keeps breaking. Or, the person needed to complete a task keeps coming in late, can never be found, your people have complained, and leadership hasn't addressed the issue. Or, your employees have offered ideas to evolve the process, asked for further training, etc … and nothing has been provided. Sound familiar? As a leader, be sure your people have the tools, coaching, and opportunity to not only hit the quota but to blow it out of the water with as little friction as possible!

Remember, the positive of a quota is people know "the number" and are on the same page. Leadership is examining the quota, allowing it to evolve, and providing your people with the proper tools needed to succeed!

### The 2 BIG Concerns!

The first BIG CONCERN of a quota is that it's limiting and not as functional or inspiring as most organizations may think. Yes, it provides a set number to determine "Success" … however, let's take a brief look at the 5 Types of Employees.

"The Inspired & Motivated" within your organization were going to meet the quota and beyond anyway because that's who they are! "The New & Unknown" will do the pace of those they partner with or were initially trained by; therefore, get your "New & Unknown" around your "Inspired & Motivated" quickly and often. Your "Steady Steams" are your reliable workers … let them know the number and they tend to hit it. "The Here, but Not Here", have dreams outside of the company or may actively be working on getting fired … the quota may not mean much to them at all. Lastly, "The Grouches", may not care about the goal … or they'll hit the quota with a lot of negativity, gripes, and gossip along the way.

Be Mindful … many employees outside of the "Inspired & Motivated" Type will reach the quota only to SLOW DOWN right after achieving it … or … see the quota is in sight and SLOW DOWN to pace the day. Quotas have their positive, however leaders must be mindful of this unfortunate truth!

The second BIG CONCERN of a quota is the number set becomes more important than the person or team pulling it off. As a leader, I'm sure you care about your people … I'm also sadly aware of some companies that have told their staff how replaceable they are and how quickly someone else can come in to do their job! Although this is a universal truth ... let's face it ... if you pass away tomorrow, your company will mourn; then post your job on Indeed, interview, and replace you with a few days to weeks ... a harsh truth ... but you don't say that to your people or intentionally make them feel that way! Unfortunately, quotas can inadvertently make our people feel like interchangeable parts in a machine.

Here are a few examples to be aware of ... those newly promoted into leadership positions may be hyper-focused on managing; because they've yet learned how to lead ... therefore, it's easier to focus on quotas rather than their people. Those in leadership positions for too long who have burned-out, bored-out, or are on auto-pilot may begin to sound like a robot droning on about the quota. The biggest concern regarding quotas is they can fail to motivate and inspire. So, what to do?

**The 2 W's**

*Their "Why and What"* – As a leader, stay curious about your people; knowing "Why" they work for the company, "Why" they like their job, and "What" they'd like to get out of working with you and for you?

Some of your people may mention wanting a promotion, raise, increased knowledge of the various areas of the organization, or may simply need the job to pay next month's rent. Being curious will say a lot about your leadership; allowing you to mix their "Why & What" with your goals and quotas!

*What's a "Win"* – It never ceases to amaze me how many people wake up and live their life on auto-pilot, professionally and personally. Ask yourself as a leader (every morning when you rise), what's a win for me today? Ask your team, ask your people individually, ask your kids. It's amazing what their answer may be! Saying it aloud makes it real, makes it important, and more doable!

As a leader, you now have an opportunity to help your people develop a plan or help them to evolve their answers. "What would be a win for you today?". "Awesome, how are you going to do that or make that happen". It's important to help narrow down their vague concept of a "Win" to a more reasonable, doable, realistic, and bite-sized action plan ... these actions done consistently will breed a professional and personal evolution!

I was recently driving my son to school and we had this "What's a Win Conversation". He answered, "to win my basketball game after school today". I responded, "Awesome, how are you going to do that?". He said, "Play my best.". My final question was, "What does that mean specifically?". He said, "get to my spots on the floor to take my jump shots, drive to the hole to score, pass, or get fouled, and play great defense to get steals". Now that's an answer, a plan, and the way leaders think!

*"Leadership is examining the quota, allowing it to evolve, and providing your people with the proper tools needed to succeed!"*
– Andre Young

# CHAPTER 34

## A Leader's Push; Just Because You Can, Doesn't Mean You Should Leadership!

To me, Leadership is synonymous with coaching and mentorship! The job is to guide toward the agreed definition of success by providing information and pushing (sometimes gently and sometimes with a big swift kick in the pants) a person or team past their comfort zone to achieve what wouldn't be achieved otherwise. I've been on both sides receiving this push and providing the push; as a player, an employee, in management, and as an owner! At times it can be fun, rewarding, and exhilarating; while other times, it can feel annoying, burdensome, and exhausting. At some point, you'll have to push your people and team through some tough times, crisis, and change ... but how to do it?

The biggest mistake I see when leaders and organizations begin to push through crisis and change is.... They forget to manage the ebb and flow afterward; wanting to stay at full throttle because they enjoy the pace of production and its generated revenue ... It becomes intoxicating! I've worked in companies that became short-staffed; so, everyone pitches in to get the job done ... because the job got done ... the company fails to hire extra staff and that pace becomes the norm.

As a college football player, we got a new linebacker coach my senior year. He was a great man, tough, and a Pitbull in human form! We were pushed to our limits physically during every practice. This proved great during pre-season; making us hungry, fast, and machine-like. However, as that pace continued throughout the season, I literally felt myself wear down and then start to break down. Back then, I didn't have the leadership skills I have today and as the leader of the linebacking group, I failed my team by not speaking up.

Late in the season, I was injured and missed two games. Upon my return to game action; we were in a meeting reviewing game film and coach said ... "Wow, Andre you look fast!" ... and my thought was, "Yeah, I wasn't getting murdered in practice for two weeks and had time to rest!". Yes, it makes sense as a team and an organization to always have your vision, expectations, and standards set on high. It also makes sense to know how to push and when to let up!

**Gather to Explain**

When the time comes ... not "If the time comes" ... WHEN the time comes to push a person or your team past their comfort zone, it helps to gather them to explain. Be transparent about what's going on, why it's going on, what the new expectation is, and when possible ... brainstorm ideas on how to do it to include them in the push. They may not agree or like what's going on or why it's occurring; however, they tend to appreciate transparency and having the tools to be successful! Perhaps they have an idea that blows your socks off and it only makes sense to go with it. Perhaps you help to help fine-tune their idea. Or, their idea is not a good fit and you share the bigger picture and challenge them to fit it better.

### Time-Frame It

Remember, "The Push" is meant to help succeed through a time of crisis, deadline, or drastic change ... it's time-limited; not meant to be the norm. Most managers, employees, and team members are willing to rally for the win; but when that pace becomes the norm ... people will begin to burn out at different speeds. Again, one of the saddest things is when an "Inspired & Motivated" employee burns out and leaves ... or burns out and stays! When they become bitter and stay, they begin to recruit ... and that's not good for the future of your leadership!

Set a proposed time-frame for the push ... is it a month, a quarter, a year? What's a "Win", how do we win, how long are we doing it this way, and what's the progress we're making? When "The Push" is necessary, it's important to stay connected with your people! This requires an increased connection with your staff; as in times of crisis or crunch, it's likely those in management will disconnect, fade into their office, and run the world via email. In our new remote-work world ... it's even easier to do just that.

### Reward It

"Rewarding It" sounds easy and common sense, right? Yes, it makes tons of sense to reward your people for the EXTRA they're doing to keep the organization afloat. However, be sure you're rewarding them in ways that matter for them! Receiving a texted "Thumbs Up" or a company-logoed Yeti is not the reward most employees dream of!

As leaders, brainstorm reward ideas as a group, include employees and front-line people, find out what's reasonable, doable, and fair ... and implement it. Your people are busting their butts at work and most likely taking it home with them ... if not literally ... than figuratively, as they return home or shut down their laptop exhausted, complaining to their significant other, perhaps taking it out on their kids, etc. Reward your people and their families; as they are all effected by "The Push".

### Get Back to Pace

This final piece may be the hardest; as it's so tempting to keep going. As a leader ... you want to GO, GO, GO! The organization can become Revenue-Drunk, intoxicated with making more with less people doing more work.

When "The Push" has proved successful and the crisis is adverted ... it's time to get back to pace! I'm not implying a drop-off in positivity, less attention to detail, or lower standards ... I am suggesting, you as a leader, work to lead the ebb and flow of your team and work to reset a reasonable pace for your people. For example, through the crisis, you asked an employee to absorb three more tasks, another coworker's duties, and to extend their work hours. Can this person now go back to the job they were initially doing? If not, can they receive a new title and the rewards that come with the new responsibilities ... if they want it?

The point is to get back to a realistic pace. Sometimes, the new pace may be dictated for you, as you may not be the head leader in charge. When this is the case ... the goal is to: Gather to Explain, Connect with your people, Reward It, Uphold new standards, and adjust your team accordingly; as some employees will move on, need to be moved on, and new people moved in.... But this is another topic for another time!

*"The Push is meant to help succeed through a time of crisis, deadline, or drastic change ... it's time-limited and not meant to be the norm ... Be Mindful!"*
– Andre Young

CHAPTER 35

# A Leader's Holiday, 5 Steps to Lead Through the Stop & Starts of the Holiday Season!

You know the craziness that comes with holidays; employees taking off, your vacation days, canceled meetings, rescheduled meetings, remembering where you and your team left off, and chasing to follow-up or reschedule! The list goes on and there's no more intense Holiday Time than the weeks between Thanksgiving and Christmas ... at least in the United States and depending on when your Holidays may fall on the calendar. So, how do you lead through the inevitable and enhance not only your Leadership & Work/Life Harmony, but also that of those you're leading and your clients/customers?

**Know Your Wins!**

Most organizations have a process of closing out the year; therefore, what are your wins for the Holiday Season? For me ...

let's say I have 15 prospects interested in bringing me in to present Leadership for their organization by year's end or the following year; my win for the Holiday Season is to, of course, close them all … but that's not always likely. My Holiday Season Win may become to have signed Agreements with more than half of the companies before the Holidays end. My win for prospects I'm unable to sign agreements with before the Holiday Season ends is to schedule Virtual Calls to officially meet and speak and schedule follow-up Virtual Calls post-holiday. For me, that's my Holiday Win which leads us to the next Step!

### Your Executive Assistant

If you're lucky enough to have an Executive Assistant, great for you! If you're not, no worries … the truth is, we all have an Executive Assistant and it's called your phone, tablet, or laptop. Leaders anticipate … we know the Holidays are coming, the professional chaos that comes with it, so let's not be surprised and negative about it … let's beat it!

Weeks before the Holiday Season begins, bring awareness of the upcoming season with your employees and clients/prospects. Be sure to schedule meetings in advance; place the dates and times into your calendar with alerts. I usually make my alerts two hours before and 30 minutes before; allowing you to be where you said you were going to be and maintaining your professional reputation at all times. I often place the meeting in my phone while I'm in front of the person or while a virtual call to model the behavior. Before the call or meeting ends, I like to ask, "How would you like to best move forward or when's best to meet again? I look forward to hearing what you liked and anything you'd fine-tune to best move forward. Do you mind if we schedule it now so I'm not chasing you or you're chasing me?". Feel free to reframe this question and make it your own. The point is, you'd be surprised how many leaders never ask me first ... leading to the biggest mess of "Let's circle back" with you chasing them and losing your power, or the least likely ... them chasing you ... negatively impacting your reputation as the person that never gets back to people. This leads to Step 3!

### The Inevitable Misses

No matter how perfectly you do Steps 1 and 2, Step 3 is inevitable! During the Holiday Season, the people you so intently scheduled with will cancel, reschedule, or flake. This happens for many reasons; they're as busy if not busier than you and attempting to tame their ever-growing tornado of things to do. Expected meetings and unexpected meetings continue to pile up and take over their day, they have people calling off or on vacation to make up for, their kid's school play was at 9:00am on a workday ... and the list can go on! So, what to do?

1. Know most people feel terrible for having to cancel or that they forgot. You know how you feel when you forget about a meeting, how it made you look, or that you wasted someone's time? They feel the same! Therefore, connect to make them aware you were on the call and at the meeting and understand these things can happen. You look forward to reconnecting before or after the Holiday Season, whichever is best for them and offer two dates. One date and time within the Holiday sphere; some prospects would like to include what you offer in their end-of-year planning or budget. Remember ... YOU and what YOU OFFER may be their "WIN"! Offer a second date post-Holiday and see which they select.

Keep a list of missed or requested rescheduled meetings right on your desk with their names, the date of the missed meeting, contact info, and what the meeting was going to be about. I'm honored to work with and speak with many organizations around the world and one or more will inevitably fall through the cracks as leaders ask to reschedule numerous meetings throughout the Holiday Season. It's nothing personal; simply inevitable. Remember, leaders anticipate! Therefore, maintain that physical list at your desk and be ready to reach out when the Holiday Season comes to an end; utilizing A Leader's Two Dates, as I shared above!

**Include Your Team**

As a leader and as an employee during the Holiday Season … I know you're busy! It's important to remember "Winning" isn't only about YOU. It's about your team winning both professionally and personally! Professionally … does your team know what the wins are? Do you know what winning means for them individually? How will you celebrate your team in our new hybrid world during the Holidays?

Personally … work/life harmony matters for you and your family; especially during the Holiday Season! It would be a shame to hit the mark at work and miss it at home with those who matter most. Yes, the Holiday Season will inherently involve time spent with loved ones … time we usually take for granted. By all means, do that time and enjoy that time! As a leader, can you and will you Make Time and Take Time for meaningful moments during the Holidays with your significant other, Date-Days with your children 1-on-1, and time with your friends … instead of exhaustingly preparing for the Holiday and returning back to work even more exhausted than you left! My wife and I hosted our first Annual Friendsgiving and all I could think was, "Why haven't we done this sooner?". What a wonderful time and I truly felt lucky and joyful returning back to what I get to do for a living!

## Clean-Up-Time

My 2-year-old daughter can make a mess like no other. When she colors, it's inevitable she's going to dump all of the crayons onto the floor, then become 10-Second Tom; running off to make a mess somewhere else for 10 seconds … and repeat! it's adorably crazy and crazy adorable all at the same time, Lol! When it's time to clean up, we play the Clean Up Song! If you're unfamiliar or don't have kids, you ask your Alexa or Siri to play The Clean Up Song. As soon as it starts, all kids magically stop in their tracks, start dancing, and cleaning up voluntarily … it's a true WOW moment to witness for the first time!!! Why do I mention this?

It always makes me giggle a bit when companies say, "Let's get together after the holidays, we'll be less busy then". Part of me fully understands; as there's much to do to close out the year … I get it! The other part of me knows everyone will be as busy … if not more … with their organization's Q1 goals when they return … all the while taking care of the loose ends of the previous year. Therefore, it's important to play that Clean-Up Song as a leader when returning from the Holiday Season!

Remember that list you kept at your desk of clients/customers/employees/etc. that missed or needed to reschedule their meetings. Make Time and Take Time to clean up and reconnect; as these are the people already dialed in as an asset to give you money, time, or whatever you were asking for and planning. Clean Up with your team to tie up any and every loose end. Lastly, evaluate YOU as a leader from last year … what did you do great? What would you like to fine-tune? What was your biggest mistake and what did you learn from it? What's your dream? What's your vision and Vision

Factors going into the new year? Clean-Up-Time is essential for your Leadership & Work/Life Harmony, your people, and your organization. Enjoy it, Apply it, and Evolve it!

> *"It's important to be mindful that your list is making you, your team, and your organization BETTER ... not just BUSY!"*
> – Andre Young

# CHAPTER 36

## A Leader's Assessment; The Art of Assessing Your Leaders and Teams!

Many people make fun of Reality TV ... and the joke in my home is everyone knows what room I've been in because when they turn on the TV a reality show pops up! The truth is, I love people watching and listening ... to a degree ... and there is much to be learned through examining interactions with an outside perspective. I recently watched a show where a boss scheduled a meeting with one of the company's executive leaders and asked, "Tell me about the team?". The executive's answer was negative, all over the place, and generic to say the least. Why? The question itself was lazy! As a leader within your organization, I'm sure you do your fair share of evaluating, assessing, and questioning your leaders to understand best how their team is functioning and hopefully how you can help. So, how to fine-tune this process; especially since YOU called the meeting!

**Individual Focus**

Let's go back to that lazy question and the downside of, "Tell me about the team.". Because the question is so broad, an employee responding to it doesn't know how to answer or what you want to hear. Therefore, they're likely to go on a disorganized rant that frustrates you and exhausts them, or provide too little information that makes you play 20 Questions, or they may operate off their emotion of the minute ... sharing only negatives due to recent frustration, or only positives due to recent adulation.

As a leader seeking to assess, I find it best to set regularly scheduled meetings with your team leaders. You'll have to decide what "regular" means for you. Is it weekly, monthly, quarterly? It's also helpful your employee knows "what and who" the meeting will be about; allowing them time to properly assess individuals ... rather than spouting off their emotion of the minute!

In any case, here are 3 simple questions; allowing your people's answers to enhance your leadership, their leadership, and their team:

1.  What do you like about _____(the person)_____? What are they doing great or good?
2.  What could they stand to fine-tune; allowing us to achieve our vision, enhance the team, and evolve them professionally and possibly personally?
3.  What's your plan regarding your leadership to marry what we've discussed here with what they need most professionally right now?

Remember, leaders build other leaders! The first question starts the conversation with positives; forcing your leaders to think and say something positive ... as they are used to flying around at mock speed, putting out fires, and possibly burning-out.

The second question is significant for several reasons ... it implies EVERYONE and ANYONE can get better; including your leaders! It focuses on impacting your staff as people ... enhancing their Leadership & Work/Life Harmony. Question 2 also mentions "enhancing the team" ... As a leader, it's important to keep in mind teammates may be getting projects done, but it doesn't mean people are being positive, polite, courteous, and don't want to rip each other's heads off!

The third question makes the leader you're meeting with step up and lead! They've heard themselves say the good about their employee/s, ideas to best fine-tune ... and are now challenged to come up with a plan of action ... what a powerful topic to follow up on!

For the leader exiting this meeting, it's now time to schedule and conduct 1-on-1 Meetings with your employees.

- Share the P.O.W. – The Positive of the Week – you go first!
- Ask what they want to get out of today's meeting
- Marry their goal with your new plan of action; explaining you just met with the "Big Boss" about the great things the team has done and ways to improve
- Establish a plan
- Ask, "What was your biggest takeaway from today's meeting?"

Follow Through as a leader is everything ... or else great ideas die, motivation fizzles, and plans become undone! As the top leader, be sure to follow-up and have your Assessment Meetings more than once per year in your people's Annual Review ... it will work wonders!

**Team Focus**

Earlier I mentioned your team or employees may be completing their tasks, but may want to rip each other's heads off. Of course, that will happen with any team as people share conflicting ideas, challenge each other professionally, and compete for positions, raises, etc. However, when it's happening all the time, you've got a culture problem!

In your Assessment Meeting, you've covered the Individual Focus ... now it's time to focus on the team as a whole by asking, "On a scale 1-10 (10 being the best), how's the team working together; regarding positive interaction, meeting deadlines, and coming up with new and creative ways to make an impact?". These are my Power 3 related to my Vision, Expectations, and Rules ... feel free to use your own.

Whatever the rating ... ask them to explain what the number they shared meant to them ... and start with the positive. For example, a leader may rate their team a 7; then share all the reasons the team isn't an 8, 9, or 10 ... That's negative! Stick with the positives and share why the team is not a 1, 2, 3, 4, 5, or 6!

Then, what would it take to move up a number or two? Your leader will share what they think would help the team excel, and this is important, but only 1/3 of the process. You now get to share your ideas and encourage him/her to find out their team's answer. When you marry this altogether ... that's how winning is done!

Assessments matter, ratings matter, and hopefully my Leader's Assessment has added a few new tools to your toolbox ... Enjoy!

*"Follow Through as a leader is everything ... or else great ideas die, motivation fizzles, and plans become undone!"*
– Andre Young

# A Leader's Sell; The 5 Steps to Sell like a Leader!

As a Bonus Chapter in a book about leadership, it may seem odd I'm writing about selling. At first, I thought so too! However, companies and individuals have continuously reached out to inquire about my process or asked me to present at conferences for their sales teams over the past year. I never thought of myself as a salesperson or sales guy; however, the life of a professional speaker and leadership trainer is all sales and negotiation! Suppose you were a fly on the wall following me around all day. In that case, you'd see me on numerous Virtual Calls with wonderful leaders of organizations discussing their concerns, pain points, and negotiating deals that will continuously impact their leaders and teams! The truth is … in my business, you'll do more negotiating than you ever do speaking. As an athlete, you'll practice more than you'll ever play in games. The trick is to fall in love with the process. So, how do you Sell like a Leader?

**A Leader's Product**

Product is two-fold, a product you already have or product/ content you're creating! You may work for a company that has products for you to sell. My last job as an employee, I took a sales position at Bob's Discount Furniture. Initially, it was a shot to my ego; I had my own company, twelve staff, a book next door at Barnes & Noble, and I stood there selling furniture. When you start a business, you don't make money right away ... so, I needed a job! It turned out to be the greatest gift for me professionally as I was able to apply and prove that all of my Leadership & Work/ Life Harmony concepts worked not only top-down but also bottom-up. My point is, as a salesman at Bob's, I had existing products to sell. It was my job and it's your job as a leader to learn your product and know your product ... and be able to "Romance Your Product" for the buyer. Some buyers only need to see it to love it and buy it. Others will have questions ... some a thousand of questions ... can you answer them?

The other type of product is the content you create. This is my realm, as a professional speaker and author, everything I present I've created. You may create videos, books, masterclasses, or a tangible product. Whatever you create, do it regularly, consistently, and put "Creation-Time" into your schedule! I can't tell you how many people ask me how to become a writer, get started in their business, or my field. My answer is to create content on a schedule, know your content, and schedule your content ... therefore you have a library and can create out of the honor you have for your craft and not out of stress! For example, I write once per week on Sunday mornings and record a Leadership Video once per week from the writing ... it's in my calendar ... giving me a library of content and a list of content to meet the variety of needs organizations face.

You may be asking yourself, "Do I need that much content?". No, you don't! I've heard some speakers do the same speech over and over for years. Because they've perfected it; they can charge more over the years, do it for different organizations, and say it in their sleep. They're companies that have perfected ONE THING ... and they do it so well that their name is synonymous with that thing ... and you know where to go when you want or need it! Whatever route you choose, learn your content and work to make your name synonymous with your content ... to best sell your content!

## A Leader's Network

When I was working at Bob's, I was also networking pretty heavily in my area; attending the traditional face-to-face, hand-shaking, and giving your 30-sec commercial networking events. I suddenly realized; I had a decision to make ... was I going to be Mr. You Evolving Now doing Leadership & Work/Life Harmony for organizations or was I going to be the Bob's Guy ... both could be advantageous, however, I remembered an old saying ... "The man that chases two rabbits catches none". Besides, have you ever had someone come up to you and hand you four different business cards or tell you they're involved in everything from A-Z ... it's hard to believe they're any good at one, let alone all of them. I chose Leadership & Work/Life Harmony and you will need to choose who you are, what you're selling, and why!

There are several ways to network on social media; one may be great for you and one may be great for another ... the question in this type of networking is, are you simply entertaining people or do you have a front-end and back-end process?

Whether you're using ads on social media, handing out flyers (I remember doing that!), writing blogs, posting videos etc ... The point is NOT TO SELL ... it is to GIVE!!! When I first started creating content, I was so protective of it and wanted to charge people right out the gate because I knew how precious the information was; why didn't they buy? I quickly learned to GIVE not to sell! Think of the lady that stands in the Food Court and says "You try this chicken!" You weren't even thinking about chicken, now you're interested, you eat it, and suddenly you have your whole family in line ordering platters of Honey Chicken!

As a leader and seller, BE THE CHICKEN!!! When you have a more tangible product that's harder to free-gift ... give away the knowledge you have about the product, how to best take care of it, success stories about it, etc ... making your name synonymous with what you sell and when a client/customer is ready to buy ... you're the first person that pops into their mind! The trick of sales is that YOU are always selling YOU not the product!

Don't let me get you in trouble! When networking on social media and you work for a company and want to promote their product ... be sure you have your organization's permission of what you can say, cannot say, etc. Once you have permission and clarification ... it's not about selling ... it's about teaching and mentoring! If I'd chosen to be the "Bob's Guy" instead of the "Leadership Guy", I would have created videos or blog content on tips for great questions to ask a salesperson when shopping for furniture, what to look for when ready to purchase, best measuring practices to ensure a great furniture fit in your home, and more; giving great knowledge so when they think of furniture ... they think of me ... not Bob's ... ME! Therefore, no matter where I sold furniture ... they'd always be seeking me ... and you can do the same!

Next, please understand that simply positing to social leads to entertainment not sales. The formula is to post, but have a back-end process to connect! Connect with people and prospects, reach out to say hello, and provide a short learning video to teach a tip, wait a bit, and send a request to connect ... along with another short learning video. You've connected without selling, said hello without selling and added value, requested a meeting without selling and added value ... by the time your prospect says "Yes" to a meeting ... all you have to do is be the same person you were on the video or blog! Tip: It also helps to offer two dates ... Thursday at 1:00pm EST or Monday at 9:30am EST. This will save you the numerous emails of chasing, as I shared earlier in this book.

This also holds true in the old-school way of attending physical networking events. Decide who you are and what you're promoting. Be able to say what you do in 5 seconds ... the 30 Second Commercial always made me cringe; as if anyone would want to hear you ramble on for 30 seconds introducing yourself! I say, "I'm a professional speaker and author". Then people tend to respond, "Oh, what do you speak about?". NOW we can talk!

When you meet a prospect of interest, it's not like social media where you have the time frame I mentioned above. After exchanging pleasantries an conversation, it's time to ask the simplest of questions most don't ... "It's been great talking with you and it'd be great to get together to talk more. Would you like to schedule a time to get together? I find it best to schedule while we're here (while pulling your phone out) so I'm not chasing you and you're not chasing me!" Most people exclaim, "Yeah, that's a good idea!". For me, three of those types of connections checked the "WIN" box and I was free to mingle and relax for the rest of the evening ... and connecting with anyone else was a bonus! Know your definition of a "WIN" prior to attending a physical networking event and winning is what you'll do!

## A Leader's Crown Jewel Question

When I first began in sales, I did the complete opposite of what I did when I was a Mental Health Therapist. I was either so eager, desperate, or nervous to sell I spewed my menu all over people. Then, one day it hit me ... know your products, how they best serve and impact, and simply ask the question that has become the Crown Jewel of Questions ... "What would you like to get out of bringing someone like me in?... allowing me to match it what I have, customize, create, or refer"!

I've found this Crown Jewel Question allows your prospect to relax, breathe, and respect that you may have a cure for their pain, you're willing to brainstorm to create it, or you're not simply here for a quick sale and open to referring outside of your wheelhouse. It also gives them some skin in the game; having to identify their pain points aloud! 99% of the time, they will lay out the issue and you'll know what you have that works best and what you can customize, create, or refer because what they need is outside what you do. Now it comes down to timing and budget!

## A Leader's Now or Later

When you've determined a plan of how your service will best impact your customer's needs, it only makes sense to move forward some way and some how! It may be sending a proposal, an agreement that needs to be constructed and sent, or an outright sale to be processed right then and there. The questions are:

So, how do we best move forward? Would you like to sign or purchase today or did you have another time in mind? Or, my favorite ...

When were you looking to have or do this?... Today, this month, later in the year, next year? I love this question as it allows your prospect to relax; as they often think you want their business

NOW ... and that's not always the case. This question works great for you as it allows you to book your calendar into the future. I often joke, "My family has to eat next year too, so next year works for me!". The point is, having business on the docket three months, six months, or a year from now is rarely a bad thing ... Be Mindful!

The next step is putting together a proposal and providing it to them no later than the next day. Schedule a Follow-Up date and time before ending the meeting or call using A Leader's 2-Dates. "When we talk again, it'd be great to hear what you liked about it (the proposal) and anything you'd fine-tune!". This is my favorite, allowing the customer time to review (if necessary). In my profession, I've found closing a deal takes multiple meetings anyhow ... so no need for high-pressure tactics. When I was selling furniture, high-pressure selling may work initially but isn't suitable for ongoing loyalty to you as their Go-To Person! It also allows you to get back to your definition of busy and them to go back to theirs without you having to chase them down ... and them feeling like they're being hunted!

**Follow-Up**

Imagine how difficult sales would be if you always needed brand people to buy your product. Make it easier for yourself, your business, and your organization by working smarter and harder as you Follow-Up with those that already know you and enjoy you! What a simple concept that often gets ignored due to "Busy" and rushed when it's month's end and time to fulfill that quota! As a leader, be sure to follow-up with past clients/customers, past prospects, current prospects, and recent sales. Whether it's an email, postcard, or social media direct message ... something! People who have bought from you before are more likely to buy from you again; especially when you use this strategy.

Past prospects may not have been ready to move forward when you last spoke or are now in an entirely different situation now. Follow-Up to say hello, connect, and inform. Current Prospects are as "busy" as you are and may not mind reminders from time to time. Lastly, follow-up to Thank and Say Hello to those you recently sold to; wishing them a Happy Monday or a great Holiday ... you like it when someone does it to you ... give that gift to them and be a leader you can be proud of and that they want to continue working with!

*"The idea of sales is that YOU are always selling YOU, not just the product ... Be Mindful!"*
– Andre Young

## LET'S STOP BEING "BUSY"
## AND START BEING "BETTER"!

The truth is, you can learn about leadership anywhere. You can go to your local bookstore and find hundreds of books on leadership. You can go to Amazon.com and find millions of books on leadership. So, how do I ... and how will we talk about it differently? I break leadership into two parts; personal leadership and the daily leadership skills it takes to effectively lead a team!

Personal leadership involves how you choose to show up to your work, your relationships, and your life ... in a way that makes people want to follow you because they enjoy who you are and how you are. It never ceases to amaze me how much more people will do for you, with you, because of you, and forgive about your mistakes as a leader when they have a connection with you!

Daily Leadership is the set of leadership skills it takes to effectively lead a team! So, whether you've been leading for forty years or forty minutes ... I hope you believe, as I believe, there's always room to grow and EVOLVE! Enjoy The Leader's Toolbox as you learn common sense and easy-to-use tools to enhance not only your leadership, but also that of those you're leading!

*www.youevolvingnow.com*

# ABOUT THE AUTHOR

Andre Young is a Professional Speaker, Author, Leadership Trainer, and Founder of You Evolving Now, LLC. He worked as a Mental Health Therapist for 19 years, played sports at every level from high school to professional, has been an employee, a business owner, and self-employed, and has written 4 books focused on enhancing Leadership & Work/Life Harmony.

As Founder of You Evolving Now it's his mission to enhance Leadership and Work/Life Harmony for organizations, leaders, employees, and teams with his high-energy, interactive, culture-changing leadership training programs and speaking engagements; allowing a professional and personal evolution!

# A free ebook edition is available with the purchase of this book.

**To claim your free ebook edition:**

1. Visit MorganJamesBOGO.com
2. Sign your name CLEARLY in the space
3. Complete the form and submit a photo of the entire copyright page
4. You or your friend can download the ebook to your preferred device

Morgan James
BOGO™

A **FREE** ebook edition is available for you or a friend with the purchase of this print book.

CLEARLY SIGN YOUR NAME ABOVE

**Instructions to claim your free ebook edition:**
1. Visit MorganJamesBOGO.com
2. Sign your name CLEARLY in the space above
3. Complete the form and submit a photo of this entire page
4. You or your friend can download the ebook to your preferred device

## Print & Digital Together Forever.

Snap a photo

Free ebook

Read anywhere